THE MOMENT OF CLARITY

THE MOMENT OF CLARITY

Using the Human Sciences to
Solve Your Toughest Business Problems

Christian Madsbjerg and
Mikkel B. Rasmussen

Harvard Business Review Press
Boston, Massachusetts

Library of Congress Cataloging-in-Publication Data

Madsbjerg, Christian.
    The moment of clarity : using the human sciences to solve your hardest business problems / Christian Madsbjerg, Mikkel B. Rasmussen.
        pages cm
    ISBN 978-1-4221-9190-3 (hardback)
    1. Social sciences and management. 2. Management—Psychological aspects.
    I. Rasmussen, Mikkel B. II. Title.
        HD30.19.M22 2014
        658.8'34—dc23

                                                2013031648

The paper used in this publication meets the requirements of the American National Standard for Permanence of Paper for Publications and Documents in Libraries and Archives Z39.48-1992.

CONTENTS

THE
MOMENT
OF
CLARITY

Introduction

An executive at Intel wakes up every morning with a cold dread over his body. He has spent the majority of his career working toward better laptop engineering, but he can't shake the feeling that laptops themselves will become obsolete in the next few years. Everything he is planning for the future feels wrong.

An employee at Apple senses that things have suddenly headed off course. The executive can feel a kind of disengagement. The energy telegraphs not curiosity and excitement but, rather, defensiveness. It seems like her team is turning inward, not out toward the world.

At TimeWarner Cable, an executive hears the latest numbers on declining cable subscriptions and zero-TV households. His colleagues claim it is a statistical blip, but he can't help but feel nauseous. "I know what's coming," he says to himself, "but I don't know what to do about it."

SOMETHING IS URGENTLY WRONG. You look at the numbers, you hear the presentations, you match everything up with your targets, but you know that none of it is true. Your current business strategy doesn't align with your experience in the world. Maybe you are putting all your energy into silver-bullet solutions. You might be looking over a graveyard of failed product launches. Perhaps you are leaning too heavily on marketing to make your products meaningful. Whatever the warning signs may be, the result is all the same: your business is headed off course. What do you do?

We have spent the better part of the last two decades advising companies in this very precarious state. Our consultancy, ReD Associates, has worked with groups of consumers, users, and customers all over the world, using techniques and theories from the human sciences—anthropology, sociology, and psychology as well as art, philosophy, and literature—to draw out insights too elusive to define with more traditional business tools. Why is customer behavior so difficult to understand? After working closely with *Fortune* 300 companies for almost twenty years, we have an answer to that question.

There is a set of assumptions about human behavior that drives most of our current understanding in today's business culture. We don't talk about these assumptions. Most of us aren't even aware of them. They create the invisible scaffolding supporting our surveys, our focus groups, our research and development, and, for the most part, all of our long-term strategic planning. As will be discussed throughout this book, these assumptions serve us well for some business challenges but not for all of them. And certainly not for the ones involving shifts in customer behavior. The reason for this is simple: the business culture is using the wrong model of human behavior. It is getting people wrong.

How so?

The current understanding of human behavior in business is predicated on a simple model that sees people as predictable, rational decision makers able to optimize a set of predefined preferences. In recent years, business leaders have become more aware of the limitations of this conceit. Slightly more advanced models produced within the rapidly expanding field of behavioral economics now concede that individuals are, on occasion, irrational. And yet, even these newer theories still cling to the fundamental idea that people have predefined, immutable preferences, that everything about human behavior can be understood if we only ask people what they think and feel. This idea is further fueled by the myth that all our decisions are based on conscious or semiconscious decisions. At the core of modern business culture lies the assumption that human beings are best understood by analyzing their brains and the thinking processes that go on there. Because of this assumption, businesses are ever on a futile quest to gain access to people's inner states: if we can only ask the right questions, design the right algorithms, analyze the right data set, the thinking goes, then we will truly understand why our consumers behave the way they do."

When we start to dig deeper into our own lives and the lives of everyone around us, we are forced to concede that these assumptions are wrong. The vast majority of our lives—of our so-called choices—exist below the threshold of our awareness. We are not detached; nor are we mentally aware most of the time. Think back to some of the decisions you may have made in the last ten years. When you decided to get married, did you have a clear way of articulating your value proposition to yourself? Did you create a list of pros and cons and place yourself at the center as an entirely objective arbiter in a future of your own choosing? Or did you get swept up in a mood? Did you feel compelled to make your life look similar to the lives of friends and colleagues in your community? Did you simply feel that marriage was inevitable? Why?

What about your most recent purchases? Did you buy your last car because the price-to-performance ratio was optimal? Or did you follow habit and buy an updated version of the same car that you bought five years ago, ten years ago, fifteen years ago?

How many times have you come home from the store with random things in your bag? How many times have you looked at your partner and said, "I have no idea why I bought this"? Have you ever looked back on a major acquisition or strategic choice in your own business and thought, "I don't really know how this happened"?

I don't really know how this happened.

This book has one single purpose: we want to show you that there are better ways of understanding people. We will unpack the business world's assumptions about people—whether they be consumers, customers, employees, or voters—and show you why the assumptions are flawed. And then we will use the human sciences to introduce you to a new way of understanding human behavior.

––––––––––

In the past, the human sciences were associated primarily with academia; even if a business hired a team of ethnographers or anthropologists to do product research for a new launch, seldom would their insights, or their general methodologies, go any deeper into the corporate culture. Today, however, a new method is dramatically shaping how businesses can utilize human science theories. It is coming from inside the labs of technology companies like Intel and IBM; the marketing departments of large consumer-product companies like Coke, Adidas, and LEGO; various thinkers and writers in small pockets of academic life; and new breeds of consultancies, like our own, that merge hard and human sciences. Although still in its infancy, this method is starting to show remarkable results in businesses all over the world. Our book opens up the tenets of this new method—what we call *sensemaking*—to a broader business audience. We will explain how this method—aimed at helping you better understand human behavior—can be applied to problems as varied as setting the direction of the company, driving growth, improving sales models, understanding the real culture of the organization, and finding the path in new markets.

By the end of this book, you will recognize how business culture systematically gets people wrong. And you will have a practical framework firmly rooted in theory and experience, and a problem-solving method to help you start to get people right.

The human sciences address the reality of people's lives at their most complex and, quite frankly, most interesting. Once you start truly understanding people's behavior, you will begin to see your business landscape with a new clarity. You will recognize new opportunities and identify the sources of older, seemingly intractable challenges. Such moments won't come easily or neatly—nothing worthwhile ever does—but this newfound clarity has the potential to drive the entire strategic future of your company.

Let's begin.

ONE

Navigating in a Fog

"IS YOGA A SPORT?" This question was posed by a senior vice president in one of the world's largest makers of athletic shoes during an off-site meeting in the spring of 2003. He was leading the meeting with the aim of creating a strategy for the sports performance division of the company for the next five to eight years.

The other executives were having a heated discussion about product planning, technology briefs, design strategy, sales targets, and must-win battles, but in the middle of the session, the senior VP felt compelled to bring up the question that had been plaguing him: "Is yoga a sport?" To the other executives around the table, this line of inquiry seemed to come from out of the blue. The room turned silent for several interminable seconds before the jokes began.

"Yoga—a sport? That's a good one," clucked the director of global marketing. "Okay, guys, let's finish the discussion on design strategy, and then maybe we can return to the yoga thing tomorrow before breakfast. Anyone up for some sun salutations?" Everyone laughed, and the meeting resumed. They planned strategies, pinged numbers around, and settled on the big story for 2010.

The question was deemed off topic on that particular day. Yoga was fun and healthy, but it wasn't serious.

The question, however, was.

The senior VP was feeling lost. It wasn't just yoga that was puzzling him. It was the entire culture of sport and exercise—a culture that seemed to be shifting around him. Why were so many people attending fitness centers instead of playing competitive sports? Why were the yoga classes at the local gym packed with men in their thirties while membership in local sports teams was lagging? Why did it feel as though the most popular sports activity in the United States was exercising on an elliptical trainer? And at the other extreme: what was driving millions of people to spend hours and hours a week training for extreme sports events like ultra-marathons, twenty-four-hour mountain bike races, Ironman triathlons, and adventure challenges like marathons in the Sahara? None of these were traditional sports activities, and none of them belonged anywhere in the industry's strategies.

If you don't happen to work in the sporting goods industry, the senior executive's confusion might strike you as odd. After all, it feels great to go to a yoga class or for a casual run in the park. For the majority of people in wealthier countries, participation in sports is about staying fit, feeling good, losing weight, and maintaining a balance in life.

Executives in the sports shoe business, however, see things quite differently. Just by asking the question "Is yoga a sport?" the senior VP was dismantling the core assumption driving the entire industry: *sports products are created to help athletes win.*

When organized sports took on mass appeal in the 1950s, sporting goods companies suddenly had a large consumer base of competitive athletes. The notion of competition and providing an edge drove much of the industry innovation for the next fifty years.

It was assumed that customers would choose the products best able to give them a competitive advantage. This is why so many sports companies use the language of a highly sophisticated car engine when they launch a new pair of running shoes: "the GEL-Kayano® series takes a 'stop at never' approach," with "top-of-the-line features like Heel Clutching System™ and Dynamic DuoMax®." Four seasons a year, every sporting goods company in the market launches a new running shoe with a new futuristic design element: whether it's "Dynamotion Fit," "Lunarlon and Flywire technologies," or "Wave Creation 14," every word is painstakingly chosen to communicate cutting-edge technology. If you did the math—number of running shoe brands, multiplied by the number of performance technology introductions, times the number of seasons—you would encounter hundreds of innovations in the sports shoe category every single year.

Winning is the cultural DNA of the entire sports industry—its raison d'être and for good reason. Over the last fifty years, the selling of competitive advantage has brought astounding growth in market share and profits. Companies like Nike, Adidas, Puma, and New Balance have all more than quadrupled their size since the 1980s. Until the late 1990s, the boundaries and value proposition of the business were relatively clear: although executives would tweak and improve upon their products and processes, the same fundamental equation—better performance equals winning—informed every decision. If something went wrong, it was simply a matter of tracing the steps back from that logic to discover why.

And then, all of a sudden, everything changed. It wasn't that the technical performance of the equipment had changed. It was the consumers who had changed. People were behaving differently, and no one knew why. In 2003, the senior VP sensed the change although he couldn't yet articulate its underlying causes. If yoga is a sport, then businesses have to allow for the possibility that most people don't do sports to win. By 2012—only nine years later—the market for yoga and gym clothing and other similar fitness apparel constituted more than half of the entire sporting goods market. The market for walking shoes, gym shoes, and jogging shoes had grown at double-digit rates, while the market for basketball shoes, tennis shoes, and baseball shoes was decreasing. The number of people attending fitness classes outnumbered the number of people active in organized sports by a factor of five, and more than 50 percent of demand for sports products was coming from women. According to a recent study, the top three key motivational factors for people doing exercise were positive health, weight management, and appearance. Contrast that with the key motivational factors for competitive athletes in the same survey: competition, challenge, and enjoyment. Most unexpected of all, some of the biggest innovations in exercise were not even coming from inside the sporting goods industry but were coming from outsiders like EA Sports, Microsoft Kinnect, Nintendo Wii, and Garmin.

Making the Invisible Visible

In hindsight, it is easy to see how things were changing. But step back to 2003, and place yourself inside the corporate insularity along with the other executives at the sports shoe company. Imagine the view from your office window every day: your fellow colleagues playing soccer or running along a track or biking to work. Imagine conversations over lunch while you choose from a wide assortment of performance-enhancing nutritional offerings at the company cafeteria: who logged in how many miles? What was so-and-so's time on the last 10K?

The competitiveness that had always driven innovation and strategy in the industry was explicitly and tacitly affirmed in every interaction occurring within the company itself. From the very moment
you entered the campus of the organization, professional athletes
were on display—some trying out new equipment and others there
to train for various events. During most breaks and lunches, executives didn't stay indoors at their desks eating. It was a given that the
majority of the company employees would be outside pushing themselves toward greater athletic achievement. In fact, most of them
had sought out a position at the company for that very reason: they
thrived on competition. It was the main reason they themselves participated in sports.

But that was only the beginning. The very structure of the organization favored competitive sports performance over fitness. Only
the lowest-level designers were assigned to work on training gear.
By pairing low-level creative staff with an activity like training, the
company was sending the message that sports performance was
always the greater priority. This tacit message was made explicit in
the name the company chose for training gear: "Sports Prep." Why
would anyone do yoga, or any other activity, for that matter, if it was
not a form of preparation for sports competition?

Within this company culture, everything that did not specifically
enhance technical performance in sports was dismissed as fashion,
style, or emotional. Some of these descriptions were the inevitable
result of the primarily male culture in the company. Women's interest in sports—aside from competitive advantage in performance—
was not a subject that came up organically, as so few women were
present at the strategy sessions. In fact, products for women held
so little importance to the company, they were all contained within
one single category—"Women"—that rarely attracted the best talent from the design pool. What's more, the idea of athletes being

street fashionistas, or street fashionistas being athletic, was generally regarded as irrelevant to the core competencies of the company:
"That's great, but it's just not *us.*"

The culture of the sports shoe company was like the very oxygen
its people breathed—invisible to the eye and yet an integral part
of every interaction within the organization. Understandably, company leaders were inclined to continue working with models that
had always worked enormously well for them in the past. But the
past has little relevance in the midst of an invisibly shifting cultural
phenomenon. The senior VP was asking questions that simply could
not be answered using linear and rational problem solving—*default
thinking.*

What Is Default Thinking?

We would sound naive if we claimed that companies had no clue
how to shed light on the soft factors and changes in their environment. But having reviewed and worked with hundreds of strategy
plans for some of the world's largest corporations and public and
third-sector institutions, we have learned that something is missing.
It's striking how similar to one another the strategies look these
days. The structure, language, key analysis, evidence, arguments,
recommendations—even the typeface of the graphs—are almost
identical, whether it is a beverage company, a producer of building
materials, a sportswear manufacturer, or a retail chain. It almost
seems as if what the company produces doesn't matter as long as
it is in markets where the compound annual growth rate is above
average, the capital expenditure is decent, the cost structure is on
par with the competitors, the capabilities of the organization are lev-
eraged the right way, and the value proposition is clearly defined.

Most of these strategies, created with a linear mode of problem solving, aim at getting the maximum growth and profit out of the business through rational and logical analysis. The ideal is to turn strategy work into a rigorous discipline with the use of deductive logic, a well-structured hypothesis, and a thorough collection of evidence and data. Such problem solving has dominated most research and teaching in business schools over the last decades and has formed the guiding principles of many global management consultancies. Slowly but steadily, this mind-set has gained dominance in business culture over the last thirty years. Today it is the unspoken default tool for solving all problems.

This linear mind-set borrows its ideals from the hard sciences like physics and math: learn from past examples to create a hypothesis you can test with numbers. As it uses inductive reasoning for its foundation, it is enormously successful at analyzing information extrapolated from a known set of data from the past. Default thinking helps us create efficiencies, optimize resources, balance product portfolios, increase productivity, invest in markets with the shortest and biggest payback, cut operational complexity, and generally get more bang for the buck. In short, it works extraordinarily well when the business challenge demands an increase in the productivity of a system.

But what happens when the challenge involves people's behavior? When it comes to cultural shifts, the use of a hypothesis based on past examples will give us a false sense of confidence, sending us astray into unknown waters with the wrong map.

Certain problems benefit from a linear and rational approach, while other, less straightforward challenges—navigating in a fog—benefit from the problem solving utilized in the human sciences like philosophy, history, the arts, and anthropology. We call this problem-solving method *sensemaking*.

Sensemaking: Finding Our Way through a Fog

The hard sciences involving mathematics and universal laws tell us *the way things are* and tend to take the main spotlight when we discuss our understanding of the world. This tendency is so common, we often disregard the wide range of sciences that are used to shed light on other phenomena, or *the way things are experienced in culture.* If default thinking shows us what exists in the foreground (e.g., "we are losing our market share in competitive athletic apparel"), the human sciences investigate the invisible background—the layered nuance behind what we perceive (e.g., "well-being, not competition, is the main motivating factor for many people participating in sports").

The sensemaking method is inspired by these softer sciences: disciplines like anthropology, sociology, and existential psychology as well as art, philosophy, and literature. Unlike the more quantitative and data-driven arms of the social sciences—fields of study like economics—these more humanities-oriented social sciences primarily shed light on phenomena: how do people experience the world? An anthropologist or ethnographer, for example, fits our definition of a human scientist, observing people in their own context in order to collect (qualitative) data on them. Whereas the natural sciences are focused on data with *properties* (this house has eight rooms, and that house has six rooms), the human sciences seek out data that sheds light on the way people *experience* those properties (out of her six rooms, she loved the yellow room the best of all because it was the room where she first saw the ghost of her grandmother). We call data that examines human experience an *aspect*. See the sidebar "How Do the Human Sciences Differ from Other Sciences?" for a summary of how these softer sciences differ from the hard sciences.

How Do the Human Sciences Differ from Other Sciences?

- The human sciences include disciplines like anthropology, sociology, and psychology as well as art, philosophy, and literature.
- Unlike the more quantitative arms of the social sciences, human sciences primarily shed light on phenomenology: how do people experience the world?
- The hard sciences are focused on data with *properties* (hard, objective facts like weight and distance), while the human sciences collect data that allows us to see *aspects*, or the way people experience such properties.

How we experience the world may be as important as, or more important than the hard, objective facts about the world. This is especially true for the specific set of problems where past data or scenarios no longer seem relevant.

The data driving the study of phenomena is not models or equations, but is made up of pictures, emotions, artifacts, observed behavior, and conversations. It is hard to imagine how a collection of conversation transcripts, photographs, or videos could ever support a theory with any rigor. And yet, such theories and methods do exist in the human sciences, and their analytical framework helps make invisible patterns visible. If we truly intend to understand culturally nuanced questions, the pairing of a rigorous analytical framework from the human sciences with various qualitative research methods can give us helpful insight.

Why do we need this entirely new business practice to understand our own human behavior? Think back to the senior VP. Human behavior can change—sometimes radically—and in those moments, no amount of hard data can bring the invisible factors to the foreground. Caught in this moment of volatile change, most of the VP's colleagues wanted to rely on the security of their numbers and models.

Default thinking and sensemaking are complementary navigational tools. Each is a highly effective approach suited for a different purpose. Take the health-care industry, for example, where very different methods are used for marketing established pharmaceutical drugs and for understanding why certain patients are not taking their diabetes medication. Marketing an established blockbuster drug requires default thinking: a fairly linear endeavor. It's all about efficiency, operations, and sales channels. Understanding complex patient-consumer behavior, on the other hand, benefits from a method like sensemaking. It would be foolish to suggest that a pharmaceutical company could cut out either of these methods and continue to thrive. In just the same way, most companies need both strategic modes but for very different purposes (table 1-1).

TABLE 1-1

How default thinking and sensemaking complement one another

Default thinking	Sensemaking
Hypothesis-based inquiry	Exploratory inquiry
Answers, what and how much?	Answers, why?
Research on what is and has been	Research on what is to come
Problems with lower levels of uncertainty	Problems with higher levels of uncertainty
Hard, measurable evidence	Qualitative evidence
Correctness	Truth

The Moment of Clarity

We created this book as a navigational guidebook: we aim to help you think critically about the assumptions at play in your current business strategy and to give you a radically new way to approach your toughest business problems. We take our inspiration from great philosophers and intellectuals, distilling their ideas into the practical applications of our method. We find that the tenets of the sensemaking method often feel like a relief to business executives. For far too long, despite the nagging sensation that they're oversimplifying consumer behavior, executives have turned to the same types of data and tools over and over again.

Using the human sciences as a framework for discovery is neither straightforward nor easy, but its effectiveness has been borne out in countless situations over many, many years. When executed with skill, a method like sensemaking delivers a much more profound understanding of market dynamics, akin to the dawn breaking over the horizon after a long night. *Now I see it!*

But before we can look more carefully at sensemaking, we need to critique more-traditional tools from MBA training. We might be getting all our numbers correct, so why do we keep getting people wrong?

PART ONE

Getting People Wrong

Business Analysis, Data, and Logic

The Default-Thinking Method
of Problem Solving

I'S AN AVERAGE TUESDAY. Your sales numbers are telling you that you are still making money. People are arriving at work, and your e-mail inbox is stuffed to the brim. The phones are ringing, as always, and customer satisfaction survey results are ticking in. The net promoter score needs to be improved, the launch set for next month has its usual problems, and your key performance indicators are on track. What's more, the supply chain is delayed, the R&D people are complaining that the deadlines are too short— "We need to streamline processes!"—the product portfolio is still too complex, and there are the same internal battles for budget and head count that you saw last year. Oh—and there is an organiza-tional change program under way. Again.

On an average Tuesday—most days in most companies—business executives are navigating a ship they know well along a course they have passed through many times before. This journey is not without problems, but executives know how to deal with them. Under normal circumstances, you can rely on the default-thinking method for prob-lem solving: building a hypothesis to determine what the problem is and then analyzing data to find out where the problem lies. Luckily we don't wake up every day and face a revolution. We revert to default because most days are like our ordinary Tuesday. Until they're not.

As we well know, conditions in the market shift and consumers behave in ways we cannot fathom. Suddenly we are in a fog. Is this sense of turbulent change the new normal, or will we return to sta-bility and predictability again?

Futurists and prognosticators have been asserting for decades that the current era is one of unprecedented change. In 1969 Peter Drucker, often called the father of modern management, predicted that Western society was approaching a new "age of discontinuity," where changes in technologies, markets, business operations, and the very nature of work would create an era of constant change. Alvin Toffler followed the same line of thought in his best-selling book *Future Shock*, where he described the future as a society in a constant state of shock caused by "too much change in too short a period of time." In his 1973 book *Beyond the Stable State*, the organizational learning expert Donald Schön argued that we were moving toward a society that would never be stable again. He pos-ited that companies needed to view themselves as constant learning organizations.

In the social sciences, meanwhile, influential thinkers like the British sociologist Anthony Giddens and the German sociologist

Ulrik Beck described the acceleration of change as a late stage of "modernity"—a world where not only technologies and companies, but also the very fabric of society itself, are under constant change. These ideas took hold and ushered in a cadre of business writers like Tom Peters and Gary Hamel who made change management a new management discipline in itself.

So what is mere hype about change? Although these aforementioned thinkers all have some amount of intellectual credence, it's important to view their arguments within the greater historical context. We are forever in the midst of change, but not all of it is seismic. It's vital for a business to understand the difference between the uncertainties present on an average day and the uncertainties of a major cultural shift. Anthropologists and other human scientists refer to differences in the scale of the problem: problems start out simple with known solutions and grow increasingly complex and confounding. Business issues can be categorized along a problem scale within three levels of complexity. This framework is useful for distinguishing very complex problems from those that are actually manageable. Think about your own business situation, and try to classify your problems within one of the following three levels. Instead of viewing change as the norm, the scale allows you to assess the type of problem you have: is it a problem you know how to solve, or is it a problem that requires entirely new thinking? The following list will help you classify the level of complexity of your business problem:

Three Levels of Business Problems

1. **A clear-enough future with a relatively predictable business environment.** You know what the problem is, and you can apply a proven algorithm to fix it. "If I invest $1 in media spending for advertising, I know that I will get something

like $1.5 back because of market stimulation." "The industry has average admin costs of 8 percent of total revenue. Mine are 10 percent. We should cut that back."

2. **Alternative futures with a set of options available.** You have a feel for the problem and might have seen something like it before. It makes sense to test your hunch as a hypothesis. For example, "Our sales numbers are down even when we invest in more salespeople, but we have seen the same pattern in the European Union and China. We might be hiring too many new salespeople too quickly and expecting them to deliver the same payback that the existing salespeople are delivering."

3. **High level of uncertainty, with no understanding of the problem.** You simply don't know what the problem is, let alone the solution. You can see that something is wrong, but have no clear idea about what to do. For example, "Our media division is losing business to internet start-ups," "We are investing more in customer service, but our customers are becoming increasingly dissatisfied with us," and "We are designing products that seem right for the marketplace, but the marketplace isn't interested."

The scale shows that most problems belong in level 1 or 2. These are by far the most common type of problem. Typical questions at this level might include the following:

- Are we losing market share for obvious reasons that we can do something about?

- Where are we making the biggest profit?

- Can we reduce the cost of operation?

- What does our portfolio of products look like?

- Is our customer satisfaction up to industry standards?

- Can we increase the productivity of our sales force?

- Which market segments are most profitable?

- How can we increase the speed of our supply chain?

- Do we have the right mix of sales channels?

Problems like these might feel as if they are extremely complex and fraught with uncertainty, but are they so uncertain that you have no idea how to start solving them? Are they so uncertain that you cannot even see the real problem? Do you lack the words even to describe the change?

The fact that a business problem is relatively certain does not make it trivial. Solving the problem still requires a lot of analysis, a high level of skill, many years of experience, and great operational capability. But there is a proven method for the solution—what philosophers call a heuristic—and you can have confidence that it will work.

But what about problems for which you don't know the variables and have no heuristic to hold on to? Hundreds of tools and ideas have been developed to address situations with extreme levels of uncertainty—including two of the more well-known methods: scenario planning and trend spotting—and they are often brought out to inspire thinking and strategy. Yet, even in the midst of extreme uncertainty, business leaders rarely diverge from default thinking. In this chapter, we will explain why this kind of problem solving is particularly ill suited for analyzing shifts in consumer behavior— that is, for level 3 problems. Let's look more carefully at how default thinking works.

How Default Thinking Works

The default problem-solving model has its roots in what can be called instrumental rationalism. At the heart of the model is the belief that business problems can be solved through objective and scientific analysis and that evidence and facts should prevail over opinions and preferences. To get to the right answer, so the thinking goes, you should adhere to the following principles of problem solving:

1. All business uncertainties are defined as problems. Something in the past caused the problem, and the facts should be analyzed to clarify what the problem is and how to solve it.

2. Problems are deconstructed into quantifiable and formal problem statements (issues). For example, "Why is our profitability falling?"

3. Each problem is atomized into the smallest possible bits that can be analyzed separately—for example, breaking down the causes of profitability into logical issues. This analysis would include "issue trees" for all the hundreds of potential levers for either decreasing costs or growing revenue (customer segments, markets, market share, price, sales channels, operations, new business development, etc.)

4. A list of hypotheses to explain the cause of the problem is generated. For example, "We can increase profitability by lowering the cost of our operations."

5. Data is gathered and processed to test each hypothesis— all possible stones are turned and no data source is left untouched.

6. Induction and deduction are used to test hypotheses, clarify the problem, and find the areas of intervention with the highest impact, or what is commonly called "bang for the buck."

7. A well-organized structure of the analysis is deployed to build a logical and fact-based argument of what should be done. The structure is built like a pyramid that develops the supporting facts, some subconclusions, and an overall conclusion and then ends with a prioritized list of interventions to which the company should adhere.

8. All proposed actions are described as manageable work streams or must-win battles for which a responsible committee, or person, is assigned.

9. Performance metrics and a proposed time frame with follow-up monitoring are put in place for each committee to complete the task.

10. When all work streams have been completed, the problem is solved.

When executed well, default thinking has a pristine beauty to it. In the midst of human complexity, it is tempting to believe that businesses can obtain a clear picture of what is right and what is wrong, to take opinions, beliefs, feelings, doubt, and confusion out of the equation by focusing on the "pure facts." As one of our colleagues once told us, "Give me a good McKinsey, Boston Consulting Group, or Bain, and I can solve any problem."

This idea of management as a type of applied science and technical discipline is not a recent invention. In fact the idea has grown on us for about a hundred years. It can be traced back to the nineteenth century, when *positivism*, the prevalent philosophy of the day, argued that you could objectively measure reality. The tenets of positivism can be seen in all the great art of the age: Flaubert's painstaking realism was an attempt to capture real life—the simple country medicine of Dr. Bovary, for example, unadorned and as is— while American realist painters like Homer and Whistler focused attention on everyday objects and subjects such as a rowboat or the artist's mother, shunning the adornments and embellishments of the Romantic era. In the world of business, positivism fed into the production-oriented culture that was developing as companies focused more on higher productivity and margins. Business was conceived of as a series of transactions that could be atomized and optimized. And human beings were considered rational optimizers who would engage in this transactional behavior to fulfill desires. It did not matter if the product was french fries, flutes, or fine diamond rings; the management of business became a matter of rational and linear analysis of systems: how do we move merchandise around in the most expedient way?

The founding father of management science, Frederick Winslow Taylor, was born in 1856. Taylor left a prestigious education at Harvard to work at steel companies throughout Pennsylvania. Whereas most manufacturing and factory plants had cobbled together their organization through rules of thumb and common sense, Taylor was the quintessential positivist, seeking scientifically validated measurements, or *properties*. He followed workers, clicking his stopwatch every time they started and stopped, measuring the time it took to complete each discrete action of hauling their large iron ore loads. Through his enormously successful tenure at steel companies, he extracted generalized principles of management that he used to create the world's first business case study. It wasn't long before a partnership between Harvard's School of Applied Science and its brand-new business school came calling. Might Taylor bring together his experience into something the school could teach its young students about productivity? *Taylorism*, based on the following premise, was born:

> To work according to scientific laws, the management must take over and perform much of the work which is now left to the men; almost every act of the workman should be preceded by one or more preparatory acts of the management which enable him to do his work better and quicker than he otherwise could.

The challenge of counting iron ore hauls seems quaint when compared with today's complex global supply chains. And yet, the general principles of Taylorism still provide the basic scaffolding of the modern MBA: the perfection of the workflow, the step-by-step analysis of behavior, the belief that people will usually work harder with financial incentives. Of course, today Taylorism on the production floor has been supplanted—first in Japan and then in the rest of the world—by the principles of "lean" manufacturing. Still, logical positivism, or default thinking, has kept its grip on most of the rest of the business world throughout the last century. Is it any wonder? Over and over again, logical positivism continues to work enormously well at delivering profits by intervening in the system to enhance productivity.

For most of us, default thinking is so familiar to us—the very air we breathe—that we are no longer able to explain it or even to see it. For that reason, if we really want to understand why we continue to get people wrong, we need to unpack the fundamental assumptions that make up the culture of most of our days. What exactly *is* our ordinary, average Tuesday?

Assumption 1: People Are Rational and Fully Informed

Are you a good driver? If you are like most people, you probably think that you are a better-than-average driver. A famous study by the Swedish psychologist Ola Svenson showed that more than 90 percent of people in both Sweden and the United States thought of themselves as better-than-average drivers. A similar study some years later asked business executives how good they were at running their business. Again, a vast majority of the business leaders told the researchers that they were better at running their business than the average business executive. Mathematically speaking, 90 percent can't be better than average, so either people in the survey were not telling the truth or they simply had no informed way to answer the question.

Svenson's study is an illustration of what happens when you reduce something nuanced and complex—like being a good driver—to a simple and measurable question: are you a better-than-average driver? The study shows that people have no idea how their driving compares. In the same way, most people often don't have a clue which washing machine they prefer, how much organic food they buy, which brands they trust, how good the service is in a store, or what type of coffee is the best. People may have opinions about these matters—just as they have an opinion about their driving skills—but they don't *know*.

One of the unintentional consequences of solving problems by testing logical hypotheses is that you are forced to assume that people are rational decision makers: aware of their needs, fully informed of all their choices, and capable of making the best choice. The reason is simple: it is very difficult to test a hypothesis about things that you can't measure objectively. It's even harder to test something that is deeply personal, cannot be decoded into explicit descriptions, and requires a lot of interpretation. Think about the question "Are you a good parent?" or "Do you have good taste?" A simple answer misses most of what matters about parenting and good taste.

To deal with this problem, companies base their problem solving on what *can* objectively be described, quantified, and analyzed without too much interpretation. In 2011, more than $18 billion was spent, globally, to understand consumers. The vast majority of this money was spent on studies where people were directly asked about their wants and opinions: quantitative surveys, focus groups, conjoint analysis, perception analysis, brand tracking, and customer satisfaction questionnaires. But what are all of these studies saying about the actual human experience and reality?

We did an interesting experiment recently. We wanted to understand which aspects of humanity were revealed when people were asked directly about their opinions, behaviors, taste, choice, needs, and so on. After examining hundreds of market research studies, we found that only two aspects were revealed: perception and desire. Most of these studies based their conclusion on the respondent's perception of reality. For example: "Which of the following snacks has the best taste?" "How much more would you buy of product x if the price were 20 percent lower?" and "Do you agree that organic food is healthier than nonorganic food?"

Alternatively, the studies looked at people's desires: "Which brand do you prefer?" "What type of car do you want?" "What kind of party host are you?" and "How would you like your home to look?"

There is nothing wrong with asking people about their perception and desires—it can be quite revealing and insightful—but are perceptions and desires the only two aspects of humanity that matter? And even if we decide that they are, does this kind of market research give us any understanding of how they work?

We do sometimes have very clear ideas about our perceptions and desires. Some of us even do a lot of research when we are going to make a large purchase, but these people tend to be rare. Even the most frugal and cost-conscious among us seldom fully understand what we want, much less fully understand the marketplace. Even rarer is the consumer who knows exactly what he or she wants and who then actually goes out and buys that very thing. Most recent studies evaluating how people buy reveal us to be far more chaotic creatures. We rarely know what we want. We almost never fully grasp the market and, most important, we almost always buy something at a different price than what we thought we would. Even studies of people with written shopping lists (milk, eggs, apples, etc.) reveal that they find themselves far astray from their original intentions once they reach the grocery store.

Among the three observed types of consumer situations involving intentions, each has a different degree of rationality and information. The business community focuses most of its attention and research money on the first type of situation. Although this type is the easiest to study, it is the least relevant for understanding consumer behavior.

Fully Aware Intentions, Fully Implemented

You know what you want, you understand the market, and you use your knowledge to purchase it: "I know I want collapsible Ray-Bans. Now I just need to find the best price and easiest delivery." This is the kind of intention you can study in a survey or focus group. The informant will be able to talk about his or her needs with clarity and answer questions correctly.

Fully Aware Intentions, Implemented in Unexpected Ways

Over the past fifteen years, the six-burner gas stove and granite countertops have become essential symbols in millions of American homes. They signify gourmet family dinners and tell a story of a home in balance. The reality is that such showpieces are rarely used, at least not nearly as much as the microwave hidden away in the closet or the takeout menus taped to the fridge.

People think they cook a lot, but they really don't. It's not that they want to lie to other people; they are simply lying to themselves. Surely there are segments of the market traipsing around the farmers' markets and whipping up homemade ice cream, but they are few and far between.

Take the car as another example. Buying a car is a big deal for many families, and it often involves extensive research before the purchase. But if you study how decisions are actually made, a highly complex bargaining process in the family often determines the actual purchase. People will articulate their key criteria for a car, but end up with something completely different just because it "felt right" or "my wife liked it."

In the world of hi-fi electronics, the sales force even utilizes what it calls the WAF, the wife acceptance factor, when promoting a TV or stereo. The man of the house might have one intention about what to get, having spent many evenings studying the appropriate decibels and megabits. But when it comes down to it, he ends up getting something that works in his home with his family. To put it simply, there is often a vast distance between what people say and what people do—at times, comically vast.

No Real Intentions, Lots of Implementations

Even though many companies think that sugared drinks, hi-fi systems, or even politics are the most important things in the world, we have yet to meet a company that didn't overestimate consumers' interest in its product or category. Consumers simply care less about oral care than do the people working in oral care companies. Or tennis shoes or furniture. It's not that people don't care about anything.

They just don't care as much as most companies assume that they do. And most often, people couldn't care less. When they buy one kind of chocolate bar rather than another, it is rarely because they have a strong brand preference. More often than not, it is because the chocolate was closer on the counter, it had a color that fit the mood, or it simply came packaged as a "two for one." The good news for companies is that we buy a lot of stuff. The bad news is that we don't always know why.

Assumption 2: Tomorrow Will Look Like Today

How often have we heard that some aspect of default thinking will lead us out of the dark, medieval ages of business into a modern scientific era of optimization? Common sense, popular belief, years of experience, and gut feelings might have been used in the past, but all this is being replaced by the shining light of scientific rigor and objective truth. A good example of this attitude can be found in a 2006 article in the *McKinsey Quarterly*. In identifying trends that will shape the business environment, the article says that management itself will shift from an art to a science:

> Long gone is the day of the "gut instinct" management style. Today's business leaders are adopting algorithmic decision-making techniques and using highly sophisticated software to run their organizations. Scientific management is moving from a skill that creates competitive advantage to an ante that gives companies the right to play the game.

Apparently the world has now become so turbulent and complex that managers can no longer run a business using their deep industry knowledge or general experience. Instead management itself will become akin to the computational sciences.

This view that management is a kind of technology based on scientific principles is widespread in today's business thinking. "Science has revolutionised every discipline it has touched; now it is marketing's turn," reads the back cover of the book *How Brands Grow*. The psychologist Paco Underhill uncovers the "science of shopping" in his best-selling book *Why We Buy*, and writer Kevin Hogan tells us how to influence others in just eight minutes through *The Science of Influence*.

When thought leaders use the word *science* to describe a business discipline like marketing, retail design, negotiation skill, or strategy, we are led to believe that these disciplines can be predicated on scientific truths. Does the science of shopping have the same universal laws as Darwin's theory of natural selection?

Let's consider an example. A publishing house knows, from precedent, that if Barnes & Noble agrees to put a particular book on a table at the front of the store—versus spine-out on a shelf in, say, the business book section—book sales can skyrocket by 100-plus percent. Starting with such statistical tools and a clear-cut hypothesis about improving margins is far more orderly than getting lost in the messy process of collecting data that feels incomprehensible. And it works enormously well in lower levels of uncertainty. Rarely do we have to ask, "Where does the hypothesis come from?" But by assuming that the hypothesis is based on some kind of universal law, we fool ourselves into believing that the assumptions of the current moment will also hold true in the future. In these situations, the idea that management is a kind of natural science blinds us rather than enlightens us.

A good example is the attempt to make the discipline of branding into a science. In 2003, the authors of the article "Better Branding" claimed to have invented a new and scientific approach to creating strong brands. "Marketers rely too much on intuition," they write.

"The key to building brands more scientifically is to combine a forward-looking market segmentation with a better understanding of customers and a brand's identity." The authors go on to argue that in today's business environment, it has become difficult to stand out as a brand. Spending more on marketing will be a waste of money, they tell us. Instead marketers should apply sophisticated scientific techniques to understand the needs of customers and the identity of the brand. "In short, reaching the next level requires a more rigorous, data-based edge to branding."

So far, so good.

The technique of scientific branding, we are told, is to grind the wealth of data on recent consumer trends and to find new trends that will create profitable consumer segments in the future. For example, the authors contend that the growth of the Atkins diet can be used to estimate and address a completely new market segment. They claim that because fifteen million people are on the Atkins diet (in 2001), a company could predict a new growth segment of high-protein breakfasts by estimating "obesity rates, the number of Atkins books sold, growth rates in the markets that embraced Atkins first, and the adoption trajectories of past diet crazes." The authors acknowledge that such estimates are uncertain and advise the marketer to allow for an error range as large as 20 percent.

Wait a minute. Did you say the Atkins diet? Is that supposed to be the future of eating?

According to an article in the *Washington Post*—published only three years after the scientific approach to branding was invented—the low-carb fad was beginning to fade and the Atkins diet was losing its audience fast. "As Atkins became a cultural phenomenon, hundreds of companies, large and small, swept in to capitalize on the program's popularity. They created and marketed far more low-carb products than there were dieters to eat them, including mass-market style versions of pasta, cakes, cookies, bagels and many other foods that had been forbidden on the strict, low-carb diet."

By 2004, the market for low-carb diet food was cut in half, and just a year later, it completely collapsed. Hundreds of companies went bankrupt, and millions of dollars in investment into the low-carb segment was wasted.

If you had followed the advice of the "Better Branding" authors, you, too, would have been in trouble. Perhaps an error range of 100 percent would have been more accurate?

Assumption 3: Hypotheses Are Objective and Unbiased

Almost all industries subscribe to a set of assumptions about the customers, the logic of the industry, or the "way things are done here." These assumptions often inform the most basic frameworks for discussion:

- Who are our customers?

- What do our customers buy?

- What are the basic benefits of our products?

Here are some examples.

In the toy industry, the dominating idea is that children have a short attention span and need toys that stimulate their desire for *instant traction*. A toy, it is assumed, must grab the attention of the child in the store, and he or she should not need any skills to play with it. Another assumption is that physical toys are losing ground to digital toys because the former are too tedious and not stimulating enough.

In reality, when you study children—and if you read the majority of academic literature about children—you will probably reach the opposite conclusion: children are highly motivated by play experiences that require skill and mastery and that can give them a sense of hierarchy and accomplishment. Digital play is gaining in popularity precisely because it requires a very sophisticated skill set; it can be played for thousands of hours and it gives the players clear feedback with levels and hierarchies.

In a 2002 meeting with a group of executives from the Danish company Bang and Olufsen, which is a producer of high-end televisions and music systems, we suggested that it might be interesting for the company to understand how the act of listening to music was changing. Music was moving from being at the center of the home to a more flexible and mobile experience. One of the executives looked up and said, "Sure, but that is not how we do it in this industry." Interestingly, it was not the audiovisual industry that took digital music mobile. But maybe it could have been.

In hospital design, a dominating idea is that equipment like beds, lifts, slings, and baths should be designed to help the staff move patients around without getting injured. Equipment, in other words, is designed for ergonomic purposes and with the view that patients in hospitals are inactive bodies that need to be moved around efficiently and safely. With lifts designed under this assumption, it takes three or four staff members twenty minutes to help a patient, say, use the toilet.

This design imperative quickly teaches the patient that he or she is not an active part of the healing. The equipment communicates that the patient is an object that others must work around. But involving the patient in his or her mobility both helps to heal the patient faster and also decreases the number of work-related accidents for the hospital staff. In addition, it allows for a much better patient experience. If the industry based its designs on the assumption that people are not just bodies—rather, active agents in their own healing process—hospitals would look very different.

Many companies have developed a set of assumptions about the world's geography. In the old days, the globe used to be divided up into Europe, the United States, and "ROW," or the rest of the world. This, of course, created major biases in investments and talent deployment. Today most companies have moved beyond such classifications, but they continue to have an APAC region (Asia Pacific, China, and Australia). While this group may be related geographically, the lumping together of the second-largest developed country in the world with the two largest BRICs, as well as sui generis Korea and Singapore, leads to a very shallow understanding of how various parts of the region really work. The result has been a systemic underinvestment in capital, people, and time.

The French anthropologist Pierre Bourdieu coined the term *habitus* to describe the somehow hidden but always present dispositions that shape our perceptions, thoughts, and actions. In his view, many things that we regard as common sense are in fact shaped by the social context we are in. Over time we learn what is normal and taken as a given through our social interaction with the world—our family, our society, our friends, our work—and our perceptions become a kind of automatic understanding of the world. This understanding enables us to act normally without really thinking about it.

Over time, companies similarly create commonsense ideas about the world. Certain things are simply taken as a given, no longer contested: for example, the idea that designers and engineers will never see eye-to-eye, or that open offices provide more opportunities for collaboration.

In a meeting with a marketing director of a health-care corporation, we were discussing how the company could approach the growing but very uncertain markets in China and India. We posed a question: should the company approach the different market segments in China and India in different ways? In less than ten minutes, the marketing director had taken our question for discussion and solved it with a hypothesis. He went to the white board and drew six criteria that the company could use to segment a market: size, price, channels, geography, finance, and customers. Then he created a little pie diagram for each of these factors and asked the meeting participants to fill out the pie diagram rating the relevance of each criterion. One by one, the pies were filled out and then the right segmentation model was chosen. In the time it takes to drink a cup of coffee, they had generated a hypothesis about how to segment both markets. This framework would be the guide for all of the quantitative analysis to follow. All of this proceeded according to their commonsense assumptions about marketing despite the fact that no one in the company had ever worked in either China or India.

A company might think that it has created an objective set of possible hypotheses to test. But in reality each hypothesis is always based on something. Very often, that thing is a product of culture, not of science. And once our assumptions are firmly rooted in our cultural understanding, they have a way of becoming ever more entrenched. People tend to seek out opinions and facts that support their original beliefs and hypotheses. Cognitive psychologists call this *confirmation bias*, a phenomenon that can manifest itself in three ways. First, it can bias the generation of the hypothesis when we choose a theory that supports an already existing conviction. Second, it can bias the evaluation process. We often quickly accept evidence supporting a preconceived hypothesis, while we subject contradictory evidence to rigorous evaluation. Third, it plays games with our memory. We tend to remember only those facts and experiences that reinforce our assumptions, a phenomenon psychologists refer to as *confirmatory memory*.

All of this means that our hypotheses are almost never based on objective truth. Although it can be disorienting to recognize these issues of bias, an awareness of the problem can ultimately help us. It encourages us to question everything on our quest toward moments of clarity. In Leo Tolstoy's nonfiction magnum opus *The Kingdom of God Is Within You*, he writes: "The most difficult subjects can be explained to the most slow-witted man if he has not formed any idea of them already; but the simplest thing cannot be made clear to the most intelligent man if he is firmly persuaded that he knows already, without a shadow of doubt, what is laid before him."

If you are not open to questioning even the most basic assumptions about your company and your customers, then you risk missing the new ideas that will be the future of your business.

Assumption 4: Numbers Are the Only Truth

You don't have to spend much time in the headquarters of corporations to find out that numbers matter a lot. Most businesses are downright obsessed with quantitative analysis. Forecasters spit out growth forecasts based on large quantitative models, and strategists suggest directions the company should take on the basis of quantitative forecasts of markets and growth. R&D people decide on the technology roadmap after looking at the investment calculus of the net present value of alternative investments, while marketers decide on the positioning of the brands in light of quantitative surveys of consumers in different markets. Today it is next to impossible to make any decision without the numbers to back it up. Even the reception desk is not immune to the worship. It is not uncommon to see large-screen TVs in lobby areas showing the second-by-second upticks and downticks of the stock price. Quantitative analysis is the heart of the default problem-solving model and the soul of most strategy.

It has become so dominant that companies tend to forget that the world consists not only of quantities but also of qualities. Roger

Martin, the dean of Rothman School of Management, argues that companies will simply lack ability to find the full potential of growth opportunities if they only focus on quantitative models: "The greatest weakness of the quantitative approach is that it decontextualizes human behavior, removing an event from its real-world setting and ignoring the effects of variables not included in the model."

Default thinking catalogs the world into properties: how big is the market, how many people will buy our products, how many people know our brand, which category is growing fastest, which geography is the most profitable, which customers have the highest loyalty and what technologies have the highest adoption.

All of these are good questions that can be answered with numbers, but each also has a qualitative side that might also be revealing. For example, it is good to know that x percent of your customers are satisfied with your company, but you also need to know what the experience of interacting with your company is like. It's helpful to know that x percent of the population has a smartphone, but how are people using the technology? Maybe you know that two hundred million Chinese people are moving into the middle-class income bracket, but do you know what it means to be middle class in China?

As consultants, we have experienced firsthand how numbers take on a near magical status in companies. We once mentioned to a CEO that in our experience, around one in three innovation projects failed. This was a quick estimate, which we offered up as a piece of anecdotal evidence. Weeks later, we discovered that our guesstimate of one in three had turned into "30 percent." It had become a magical number in the firm's R&D department. It was then described in the firm's technology roadmap as a fact. Everybody was referring to the "30 percent failure rate." There was even a calculation rating the risk factors in a particular innovation project and how far this particular project was from the average risk (30 percent failure).

The 30 percent figure, a tiny part of a bigger conversation we were having about innovation, was not very important in the broader context. But because it was the only thing quantifiable, it became the thing that mattered. Somehow the company was much less critical about quantifiable observations than it was about qualitative insights.

When a company is in a situation that is highly uncertain and ambiguous, the compulsion to quantify everything can become counterproductive. Quantification tends to give you one right answer. And by building on data that is already available, it doesn't give you any insight into what is really going on in the moment. It is particularly problematic when companies try to approach the future with a quantitative analysis approach. Almost all data analysis is about crunching numbers from the past and extrapolating these numbers into the future. For obvious reasons, the past does not include data on things that haven't happened or ideas that have not yet been imagined. As a result, data analysis of the future tends to underestimate or even ignore past events or conditions that can't be measured while *overestimating* those that can. Nowhere is this more visible than in business case studies.

Most business cases try to estimate the future value of a product by forming a set of assumptions about the future customer, the market, and a number of other factors. This enables the company to prioritize which projects to support and which future to eventually approach. For example, you might try to calculate the future market for a new type of protein drink. To estimate the future value, you make several assumptions about which customers would want this product, how much they are ready to pay, what year you will launch the product, how quickly people will adopt the product, how big your market share will be, and so on. Once the assumptions are in place, you basically find exciting data about these things and try to estimate a future market value by simply extrapolating the current data into the future through the lens of your assumptions. The result is often an exact number about how big the opportunity is, usually quoted in very precise figures like 347.5 million euros. The business case is presented in a well-structured, logical, and convincing format with lots of tables, graphs, formulas, risk assessments, and other signs of quantitative reliability. When you see a business case for the first time, it is the strategy session version of a steel cathedral: solid, impressive, downright irrefutable. But if you look at the *qualitative meaning* of the business case and its calculations, you often discover that it is a steel cathedral built upon quicksand.

Simply changing a few of the business case assumptions can radically transform an incredibly good idea into a complete disaster. Change the definition of the customer, the assumption of how fast customers will adapt to the new product, the historical starting period, or one of the often hidden variables factored into the spreadsheet, and the whole thing falls apart. Despite all of this speculation, the business case is often presented as a pure fact, something that is precise and predictable. A very senior executive at a drug company was organizing clinical trials for a new business case. He told us, "Tell me what answer you want, and I can organize it to appear."

He was offering facts, or properties. The numbers would all be correct. But do you want to base your business on those numbers?

In our view, the quantitative obsession leads to a sorely diminished approach to future planning. It tends to be conservative rather than creative because it implicitly favors what can be measured over what cannot. This can give companies the sense that something is big just because it is measurable—the Atkins diet, for example—while making companies underestimate phenomena not yet quantifiable, such as mobile music. Which one proved to be the more exciting innovation of the twenty-first century?

To embrace the future, *quantifiable* is not the only important point of view. *Qualitative* is important, too.

Assumption 5: Language Needs to Be Dehumanizing

Not only does default thinking offer a poor understanding of what it means to be human, but it also changes how people in companies see themselves and widens the distance between corporate life and "real life." Business and management science has become a world in itself, and the language of business has become increasingly technical, introverted, and coded. You don't fire people anymore; you "right-size the organization." You don't do the easiest things first; you "pick the low-hanging fruit." You don't look at where you sell your products; you "evaluate your channel mix." You don't promote people; you "leverage your human resources." You don't give people a bonus check; you "incentivize." You don't do stuff; you "execute." You "synergize, optimize, leverage, simplify, utilize, transform, enhance, and reengineer." You avoid "boiling the ocean, missing the paradigm shift, having tunnel vision, and increasing complexity." You make sure that "resources are allocated to leverage synergies across organizational boundaries and with a customer-centric mind-set that can secure a premium position while targeting white spots in the blue ocean to ensure that there is bang for the buck." It can become almost poetic.

The German philosopher Jürgen Habermas has developed an extensive analysis of what happens when technical language outstrips the language of everyday life. He argues that the change from a normal, everyday language to a technical, specific language suggests a shift in power. When technical language conquers simple language of the every day, it is a sign that the *system* is gaining ground and everyday human reality, what he calls the *lifeworld*, is losing ground. He goes so far as to call this shift a colonization of the lifeworld; everyday life being colonized by a force of bureaucratization and rationalization that it cannot defend itself against. Such a shift leads to a far more systematic, rule-based, and technical idea of the world. It widens the gap between who we really are and the systems that we have become.

When medical students are trained to do surgery, they go through a procedure where language is used very deliberately. To create an emotional distance between the young person doing the surgery for the first time and the cadaver on the operating table, the students are taught to use highly technical and medical language to make the whole situation bearable. The body is not referred to as a person, it is called "the subject." Removing the skin of the head is not called "remove the skin"; rather, the student "prepares the subject for incision." The parts of the brain are all called by their Latin names. Such complex and esoteric terminology encourages doctors-in-training to divorce any personal feelings from the scientific analysis required of a medical practitioner.

We should be grateful for professionals who use language in such a purposeful and thoughtful way. In the medical world, there is a functional explanation for the dominance of technical language over everyday language. It enables the medical profession to be precise; it gives the medical field a global, applicable language; and it helps doctors-in-training do things that are beyond the norm. But does the business practitioner need the same detachment from the human world? Why are we trying to distance ourselves from the people we claim to serve?

Despite the dominance of default thinking, most executives also readily acknowledge that it doesn't always work. In response to the perceived shortcomings of this more linear, quantitative method, many companies have also started to embrace brief sabbaticals from facts and figures. Such breaks come in the form of workshops, retreats, and breakout sessions, attempting to solve business challenges through a method that many business leaders like to call *thinking outside the box*. This approach is the photo negative of default thinking; it is based on the notion that ideas can come to anyone at any time. It values content generation over content quality, taking brainstorming to a whole new level.

Although the process can do wonders for building trust and rapport among colleagues, thinking outside the box and default thinking are ultimately two sides of the same coin. The coin atomizes the complexity of human behavior into discrete parts, neglecting the importance of holism and context. It's the coin that continues to get people wrong.

THREE

Getting Creative!

The Think-Outside-the-Box Method
of Problem Solving

T HE FOLLOWING ACCOUNT MAY SOUND like fiction, but we can assure you, it really happened, because we participated in it.

Healthy Harry Potter

"Listen up, everybody," shouted the energetic facilitator while clapping his hands loudly. "Please join your teams and start shooting off some wild ideas."

On a hot August morning in 2005, fifty selected thought leaders were gathered into a conference room. Over two days, these fifty experts—hand-selected for their varying areas of expertise and innovative problem solving—met for an exclusive workshop showcasing different ways that creativity and design thinking could solve some of the world's biggest problems. The experts included the CEO of a large Brazilian energy company, a landscape designer from London, the brand director of a multinational fashion brand, a technical director of one of the world's largest consumer electronics brands, an investment broker from New York, a Danish medical doctor, and an advertising executive from Singapore.

What happens when you put fifty of the world's most creative thinkers in a room for two days together and ask them to solve the world's biggest problems?

The workshop organizers were convinced that the results, in whatever shape they might take, would constitute brilliance. Such was their confidence that at the end of the weekend, they scheduled a presentation for the press and a select audience of investors, government officials, business executives, and academics to hear the final results.

Facilitated by one of the world's leading experts in design thinking and business creativity, the teams were bombarded with inspiration and an impressive menu of creative exercises. "For the next two days, we are all going to think and work like designers," the workshop leader told the participants. "We will force ourselves to think outside the box, dive deep into the user's universe, open up our minds, think big, sketch hundreds of solutions, and prototype the best of the ideas so they can be realized as fast as possible."

The teams were given a designated work space decorated with mobile walls in bright colors, beanbag chairs, bar stools, flip charts, lots of sticky notes in various colors, and, on the walls, some posters giving the participants advice and encouragement. DON'T KILL IDEAS, one poster read. Another poster asked participants, HOW DO YOU FEEL? and a third encouraged the participants: BE PLAYFUL, HAVE FUN AND GET ADVENTUROUS.

With everyone sitting in an awkward semblance of a circle, the facilitator encouraged the participants to open up and accept that the next two days were going to be outside the comfort zone: "Every one of you was born a creative genius. You have been taught to tame the creative child inside you, but he is still there. Over the next two days, we are going to let him out to play."

Groups were assigned, and world problems handed out on index cards. The team was tasked with designing radical new ideas to solve the world's health-care problems. Such a task might have seemed daunting, but the team started the day with buoyant optimism. To spark their creativity, an actor had been hired to energize the troops. She did exercises to break the ice and make the participants loosen up.

"You are not going to get any crazy ideas if you hide behind your business suit and stick to your normal rational logic," she said. "As an actor, I know that to be creative, you have to shake things up. Let's start by all giving each other warm hugs."

This request, despite the high spirits of the morning, was met with less enthusiasm. Awkwardly, arms encircled arms as people did their best to avoid touching one another.

"Wasn't that a great feeling?"

Some of the participants nodded. She pointed up at the poster that read HOW DO YOU FEEL?

"Wouldn't it be great to start every day this way?" she asked. "Just going into the office in the morning and giving each other a warm hug? I am sure we would have a lot more creativity in business if that happened."

She then opened a bag and took out an object. It was a potato. She asked the group to stand in a circle and pass it around like a sacred object: "This is not a potato. It is a magic object that you can use to get new ideas. Just force a connection between the world's health-care problems and the potato, and see what that gives you. I'll start."

The actress took the potato and considered it.

"I am thinking that the world would have far fewer sick people if we just ate more vegetables," she said.

The facilitator quickly wrote these words on a sticky note and posted it on the wall. "First idea is up!" he said. "Let's celebrate!"

He started clapping his hands, and the participants reluctantly followed. On the note, in all caps, were the words EAT MORE VEGGIES.

Now it was time for the participants. The first up—a financial investor—clearly had problems connecting the potato to the world's health-care problems. He struggled and almost faltered because the so-called creative space felt tense and fraught with consequence. He simply had to say something.

"Potato starts with P . . . Parkinson's, polio, pandemic, panic," he whispered. Then he looked up, struck by lightning. "Got it! *Patients!*" he shouted, perhaps a bit too loud, and visibly relieved. PATIENTS FIRST, read the sticky note.

After just thirty minutes, the team had produced no fewer than fifteen ideas on how to solve the world's health-care problems, all connected to the potato.

"This is just the tip of the iceberg," said the facilitator. "Now the real fun starts. The next thirty-six hours are going to be like a roller coaster ride for most of you. We are going to go through an entire creative design process that normally takes a year. It is going to be hard, but fun."

One of the participants—a family doctor famous for his work with diabetes patients—was growing increasingly uncomfortable with the situation. He had been sitting with his arms crossed, eyes askance every time a gem of "potato logic" was uttered.

"I am not sure I follow the logic here," he finally interjected. "As far as I can see, I am the only person in this group with any background in the health-care profession. And I am by no means an expert. It is not because I don't respect the other members of the team here. But I just don't see how this group can come up with ideas to solve the world's health-care problems, when none of us has real expertise in the medical profession. I mean, we haven't even defined what the world's health-care problems are."

A shadow of disappointment and worry fell over the facilitator's face for the first time all day. "I hear what you are saying," he cooed. "Your worries are good worries. Let's write them up on a flip chart and see if we can turn them into some new ideas later today. Maybe there is a breakthrough hidden in your thoughts."

He stopped to write more words in all caps before turning around again to speak to the doctor. "By the way, don't worry about the diversity of the group. All people are creative, and the more angles we have on the problem the more ideas we can create."

The workshop continued. The team was taken to a hospital and given a tour.

"Take lots of pictures, and document everything you see," the facilitator encouraged. "Act like you are flies on the wall, and immerse yourselves into the world of the users."

The fifteen members of the group were invited to observe a patient in her bed. All fifteen of them stood in her cramped space, some surrounding her bed and others practically sitting on her windowsill, a few spilling over into her bathroom. They obediently took notes and snapped photos, all the while making their best efforts to remain unobtrusive. Flies on the wall . . .

Back at the workshop, yet another exercise was waiting for them. On the wall were two big posters displaying vague flower shapes.

"This is the flower of insight," said the facilitator.

The team was supposed to fill in each of the six petals of the flower with insights from their hospital trip. One flower poster read HEALTH CARE TODAY, while the other was labeled HEALTH CARE TOMORROW. The team members started discussing what they really saw in the hospital, trying to boil down their insights to fit on a petal.

The CEO from the energy company was quick to begin: "I think it is pretty clear. The health-care system is simply not customer focused. I bet you that a hotel has ten times lower costs per guest than in a hospital, and yet the service is ten times better in a hotel."

A number of the participants nodded, and the CEO, encouraged, walked up to the flower and wrote LACK OF CUSTOMER FOCUS on the first petal.

In forty-five minutes, the flowers were full. The health-care system of tomorrow was "patient focused" and "wired and connected." It involved "holistic health care" and reminded us that "prevention matters."

The doctor furrowed his brow when the last petal was complete. "What do these words have to do with what we saw in the hospital?" he asked.

"Good comment," said one of the other participants. "Let's write it on the flip chart."

Time for the brainstorm.

The participants went through a range of exercises called things like Saucy Thinking, Random Words, and Angel and Devil. After three hours of exhaustive, creative brainstorming, the team had produced no fewer than three hundred sticky notes with ideas. The wall was covered in a veritable rainbow of creativity.

"This is incredible," said the CEO from the energy company. "We have never had that many ideas in the entire history of my company."

But when the team was asked to vote on the best ideas and find the big picture amid the jumble of paper, the sense of accomplishment quickly turned to frustration. There seemed to be no clear pattern in the ideas, many of which were too abstract when taken out of context.

The facilitator encouraged them to write down three to five big-picture headlines coming out of the three hundred sticky notes. "It's just like solving one of those puzzles where you have to connect the dots," he said.

The first big theme to emerge was the problem of child health.

"If we can just teach our kids to eat healthy foods, exercise daily, and avoid smoking and alcohol, we will have solved a big part of the world's health-care problems," the CEO from the energy company said. The doctor finally agreed. Indeed cigarettes, alcohol, and lack of exercise could explain a lot about why people get diabetes. Other possible themes included clean water for the poor, patient-centric health care, affordable medicine to the developing world, and wired health care.

But it was eight o'clock at night, and the team was getting tired.

"Let's just choose that children idea," one of the participants suggested. Everybody agreed so they could go home.

The next afternoon, hundreds of people started to gather in the creative workshop space to hear the final results. The room looked like a veritable tornado of creativity had blown through it, with sticky notes pasted here and there, early sketches and designs on tables, beanbags—still marked with the imprints of bodies—scattered in seemingly endless piles, and quirky musical instruments and children's toys dotting the room. Everyone was waiting with anticipation to hear how the world's most creative minds would solve the seemingly intractable challenges of world health.

Over the course of the day, the health-care team had worked hard on its presentation, but had encountered difficulty coming up with any cohesive strategy. As the hour for the presentation grew closer and closer, the team members all feared they would have to stand up and give up a jumbled mess of suggestions with no real structure. Fortunately, as if by magic, one of the participants brought up Harry Potter. Suddenly, all of the seemingly random bits of material snapped together into one brilliant framing device.

How could Harry Potter help children live healthier lives?

The team enlisted some design students to help visualize the idea, and only ten minutes before the presentation was set to begin, everything came together. The solution was called Healthy Harry Potter.

The presentation was scheduled to take thirty minutes, but the team couldn't stop talking. The members were energized and excited by all of the possibilities of their design solution. One by one, people in the audience started to sneak out of the room.

There was a sigh of relief when the facilitator cut the team off. No questions. No comments. After the presentation, the remaining audience emptied the room in less than fifteen seconds. The team was standing at the front of the empty rows of chairs looking at each other with a mixture of adrenaline and confusion. What had just happened?

Nobody in the press picked up the Healthy Harry Potter concept, and as a result, the idea was born and then died in that same hour. In fact, not one of the ideas ever materialized into something that could even slightly change the world's health-care problems. Not even a thought.

But the team and facilitator agreed that it had not been a waste of time. The process was great and the ideas were new, but changing the world's health-care system needed new ideas. It was akin to asking a tanker to do a 180. In the hands of the right people at the right time and with the right resources, things could change, the team agreed.

Everyone on the team except for the doctor, that is. He had left hours earlier. He had a patient to see.

How Thinking Outside the Box Works

The case of Healthy Harry Potter seems like something on the fringes of creativity sessions in business, but it is a true story based on our own experience as participants in the health-care team.

And even more interesting, it is a totally normal way to address creativity these days. Through hundreds of interactions with some of the world's biggest companies, we have observed a clear pattern in how companies think about creativity. This same pattern is easily validated if you read the literature on business creativity, go to any seminar that has the words *design thinking, creativity,* or *innovation* in its title, or simply join in an ideation session anywhere in the world as a fly on the wall.

This pattern forms the dominant mental model for what creativity is, how it evolves, how you encourage it, and, in certain cases, how you manage it. Notice that we are not talking about the practice of creation in companies, or how companies actually create stuff. We are talking about the fundamental assumptions about creativity in business. At the core of this understanding, there is always the dialogue with default thinking. If we are rational and linear during our normal workdays, so goes the thinking of today's business leaders, then we should be, by turns, strange, mystical, unexpected, foreign, random, and radical during our creative "retreats." Let's explore five of these fundamental assumptions in more depth and look at why they are so problematic for a business in a fog.

Assumption 1: Creativity Is Strange

When someone says, "Let's think outside the box," most people instantly know what it means. Thinking outside the box has become the most popular metaphor for creativity. It is defined as looking at problems in unconventional ways and coming up with ideas that are new, fresh, and unexpected. But is it so obvious that thinking outside the box means being creative? What box? What thinking? What does it mean that something is outside?

Originally, the phrase comes from solving a very specific puzzle where you have to draw four straight lines through all nine dots that are arranged in a three-row square, without lifting your pencil from the paper. The only solution is to draw a line that goes outside the square—hence outside the box. To solve the puzzle, you need to look beyond all the obvious solutions.

In business discourse, the box no longer refers to the square formed by nine dots, but refers to the conventional frame, the normal way of thinking, including the firm's organizational routines, processes, practices, and existing ideas. Somehow the metaphor reveals a very dichotomous idea about creativity in business. There is an inside and an outside of a business. The inside is based on routines, conventions and existing ideas and is not regarded as creative. The outside means breaking the routine, ignoring conventions, fostering creative leaps, and generating wild ideas. In other words, creativity is abnormal. It is strange.

Assumption 2: Creativity Is a Process

Another very popular and common concept is brainstorming. You will often hear people using this phrase to describe a specific process of group activity where a team creates ideas in a free environment without the constraints of judgment and critique. The word *brainstorming* is used for all sorts of activities that have no real logic or structure to the conversation. For example, you can say, "Let's brainstorm a list" to indicate that you will work together and that any idea you have will get written down. Or you could say, "Is this a brainstorm or is this a meeting?" indicating that the brainstorm doesn't have a deadline and a fixed structure, while a meeting has both.

Alex F. Osborn, an advertising executive, popularized the term *brainstorming* in the 1950s. He was frustrated with the lack of imagination in his employees' ideas for ad campaigns. In experimenting with creating ideas in groups rather than relying on individual ideas, he found that group creativity dramatically increased both the quantity and the quality of advertising ideas. He used his discovery to develop a generic process for creative thinking—a process that he claimed could be used in any type of problem-solving situation. In several books he wrote in the 1950s and 1960s, he applied creative thinking to a variety of areas: children, hobbies, marital problems, jobs, health, and happiness.

Osborn was a firm believer in the idea that every single person is creative and that personal creativity can be brought out in any person through the use of a procedure. It clearly worked in the advertising industry, whose key product was creative ideas. He saw it as his call in life: to take his discovery from Madison Avenue and bring it to Western civilization: "Each of us does have an Aladdin's lamp, and if we rub it hard enough, it can light our way to better living—just as that same lamp lit up the march of civilization."

In his 1953 book, *Your Creative Power*, he coined the term *brainstorming* and introduced it as a technique that produced new ideas on command: "Brainstorming means using the brain to storm a creative problem and to do so in commando fashion, each stormer audaciously attacking the same objective."

Osborn devised a very detailed procedure on how a brainstorm session was to be conducted. His most important rule was that the problem be clearly defined before beginning: "You can't solve two problems in one session."

Once the problem is clearly defined, a brainstorming session should follow four rules:

1. Criticism is not allowed. Avoid passing judgment on ideas.

2. Produce as wild a group of ideas as possible. It is acceptable and even desirable to share really unusual ideas.

3. Quantity breeds quality. The greater the volume of ideas, the greater the likelihood of useful ideas.

4. Combine and improve ideas. Participants should improve each other's ideas and deliberately try to combine each other's ideas in interesting and surprising ways.

The promise of a technique guaranteed to produce ideas landed on a soft spot in American industry, and brainstorming quickly became known as a sensational new approach that could be used to solve all sorts of business problems; it was a new panacea. Even though Osborn clearly stated that brainstorming was only designed for a very specific purpose—group sessions with *one* narrowly defined problem—over time, brainstorming became the most popular metaphor for the creative process in business. A lot of variants have been developed—lateral thinking, design thinking, TRIZ, electronic brainstorming, etc.—but they all carry the same basic idea that creativity is primarily a matter of having the right processes and steps, allowing a group to manufacture ideas as if they were parts on an assembly line. Following this logic, it is assumed that because the process is somehow more important than the content itself, experts need never even be present. In fact, expertise and deep knowledge are seen as a potential creativity blocker in certain sessions. Robert Sutton, the author of *Weird Ideas That Work*, tells his readers: "In the creative process, ignorance is bliss."

Note the way this discourse argues for defining ideas as singular objects that can easily be noted on a list, counted like beans, or put together in new ways like LEGO bricks. Ideas are seen as modular pieces, completely separate from the person having the idea and the context in which that idea was created. These types of ideas — atomized and modular—are not painful to change or explain, as they carry a low bandwidth of information. Having an idea is free, and killing an idea carries no risk.

And because ideas in this discourse are seen as objects detached from their context, anyone can have an idea, and ideas can come from anywhere. Randomness and chance play a big part in this understanding of ideas. If ideas are just particles without any inherent meaning, why not throw some of these random chemical substances into the test tube and give it a shake?

Assumption 3: Ideas Come from out of the Blue

"Even if you're not a genius, you can use the same strategies as Aristotle and Einstein to harness the power of your creative mind and better manage your future," writes Michael Michalko in "Thinking Like a Genius." We are often seduced by the romantic notion that everyone is creative, that you need only to control the creative process and remove the straightjacket of critique and judgment for genius to be revealed.

Design the right circumstances for the lightning to strike, and like alchemy, it will. Our common language around creativity does nothing but affirm this. We say, "I had an idea," or "Let's get some ideas," as if these ideas are falling down to us out of the blue sky. An executive in one of the world's largest pharmaceutical companies decided that his management team should have such an ideation session every Friday at six o'clock, at which time they could think big and visionary thoughts. He called it, unsurprisingly, the "blue sky meeting."

The thought that ideas will come to us under the right circumstances is supported by the common myths and popular stories told about the history of ideas and inventions. It is commonly believed that Einstein discovered his theory of special relativity while driving his car home one night passing the town clock and that Darwin was hit by a sudden insight during his journeys with the *Beagle*. In more contemporary times, it is cocktail party chitchat that eBay was invented because the founder had an idea about how his fiancée could trade PEZ dispensers. Of course, detailed historical accounts of what actually happened almost always show that these common stories are myths and wishful thinking, a theme we will revisit when we discuss abductive reasoning in depth in chapter 4.

Assumption 4: Creativity Is about Radical Change

While Osborn and his followers were primarily talking about how to use creative techniques to solve relatively narrow problems like ideas for product names, we are now using words like *breakthrough*, *game changing*, *disruptive*, and even *revolutionary* to describe good ideas. This change in discourse started in the early 1990s as management gurus, business scholars, management consultancies, the business press, and even governments argued that we were standing on the threshold of a new age, poised to inherit an entirely new economy—the transition from a physical-based economy to a new, net-based one. An important part of this transition, many argued, was to change the whole framework of business from an incremental mind-set to a radical mind-set.

"For the first time in history, we can work backward from our imagination rather than forward from our past," management guru Gary Hamel writes in his best-seller *Leading the Revolution*. Hamel argues that dreaming, creating, exploring, inventing, pioneering, and imagining should make up the bulk of the manager's day. And if they do not, "you are already irrelevant and your organization is probably becoming so along with you." In other words, either you have radical ideas or you die. To succeed, you need to become a revolutionary. Hamel asks his readers to give an oath:

> I am no longer a captive to history.
> Whatever I can imagine, I can accomplish.
>
> I am no longer a vassal in a faceless bureaucracy.
> I am an activist, not a drone.
>
> I am no longer a foot soldier
> in the march of progress.
>
> I am a Revolutionary.

Companies like Enron became the epitome of this type of thinking. And though the revolutionary jargon has dampened a bit over the years, the basic idea that creativity is about radical *newness* remains with us to this day. As one of our executive clients put it, "I don't care about small, incremental ideas. I want ideas that are crazy, weird, and never ever seen before. Ideas have to be really, really new. That's creativity."

Assumption 5: Creativity Is Playful and Fun

A final assumption about business creativity is the belief that creativity can only happen in a fun and playful environment. This idea is expressed through the symbols and artifacts of creativity that you often see in connection with stories about creative companies. These same symbols and artifacts automatically appear when a company is attempting to change its image and appear more creative to its clients and customers.

If the icon of default thinking is the stopwatch, thinking outside the box is a celebration of the colored sticky note. Like ancient walls of cave paintings, the whiteboards filled with sticky notes telegraph to all observers that "something creative happened here." The sticky note detritus is so emblematic that companies often take photographs of employees surrounded by such notes, seemingly deep in creative thought. Note that you can never read what is actually written on the notes. This is because it doesn't really matter. The sticky notes themselves are the message—not their content. You would never take a picture of people working on their spreadsheets to document a company's analytical prowess. But creativity needs to be loud, colorful, and, preferably, captured in neon.

Sticky notes, of course, are only the beginning of the fun. Creative companies have Nerf guns, open offices, flip charts, beanbag chairs, bikes hanging down from the ceiling, soccer tables, ubiquitous scooters, and lots and lots of laughter. "It's now time to party," writes Chris Baréz-Brown, author of *How to Have Kick-Ass Ideas*, as he draws a direct connection between playfulness and creative genius. "So the message is, if in doubt, say '*Na na na-na na*' and laugh at the world."

Baréz-Brown's book—representative of the creative-thinking body of literature—is full of language you would find in a storybook for preschool children. The enemy of playfulness, in the author's view, is the collection of experts and people who claim to know a lot. He calls them "clever clever thinky thinky" people.

Such language subtly, and not so subtly, connotes playfulness with liberation. It plays on a sense that work is enslaving our thoughts: the office is a place where we are treated like faceless bureaucrats while our expertise and knowledge is blinding us. To be creative, we need to free ourselves from the bonds of corporate bureaucracy, expertise, and rational analysis. True liberation exists in the world of a child: open, playful, curious and spontaneous.

Lest such thinking unleash a company culture that resembles *Lord of the Flies*, most creativity literature makes it clear that organizations don't want people to be like children *all the time*. Employees should behave like children on command. Thus, creative sessions that open with a series of icebreakers, energizers, and team building exercises signaling fun and play. Such playful fun can take an almost infinite variety of forms: in one creative workshop, we were instructed to "find our inner Elvis"; in another, we were asked to be "idea rappers"; and in a third, we were asked to "body-storm," meaning "don't talk at all, just play in free-form."

The discourse of business creativity, although often absurd in its most extreme cases, clearly addresses a growing and legitimate concern with the limitations of conventional management logic. And to be fair, many elements of thinking outside the box do deliver results for companies. Brainstorming, for example, is a great tool for generating a large variety of ideas on problems that are clearly defined and have a low bandwidth—ideas for product variations, product names, company or product slogans, alternative ways to solve a practical problem, lists of user attributes, and so on. The whole setup of the creative off-site workshop—complete with icebreakers, fast idea development, and energetic teamwork—has a big impact on team performance, knowledge sharing, the sense of involvement, and just plain fun at work. But it is not useful for helping executives understand why a series of product launches failed, say, or what is to be done when an entire business is hemorrhaging money quarter after quarter, or how to understand and then bet on the future.

The problem with the thinking-outside-the-box approach is neither its intention nor its tools and processes. The essential fallacy of the approach is its promise to deliver idea generation that is fast, efficient, repeatable, simple, and risk-free. Getting people right requires a deeper investigation into human behavior as well as a longer gestation period for creative ideas. It often requires training and background knowledge or experience. And unlike the tidiness of a thinking-outside-the-box off-site workshop, it is messy. Breakthrough insights aren't manufactured like widgets in a factory. They dawn on us in nascent form, like the sight of a vague shape on the horizon. They are first present in our mind and bodies in a pre-verbal state, an inkling, a feeling. Some refer to this as the "slow hunch." Einstein wasn't satisfied with the relativity theory handed down to him by Galileo, for example. He couldn't articulate why. He just had a hunch that the holes in the theory might prove interesting if he pursued them. He created a series of mind riddles for himself: imagine man could fly through the air at the speed of light, arms out in front of him in flight while holding up a mirror. What image does the glass reflect? Is it an image of the flying man's face? Does it look normal or does flying at the speed of light change his image in some way? When someone is moving at the speed of light, what happens to the light reflecting off his retina? And what about the people watching from below? Does the light reaching their retinas change the image of the flying man as well?

For years, Einstein pondered this riddle, mulling it over day after day, discussing it with friends, trying to unravel its mysteries. After ten full years, his once-vague feeling began to take a more concrete shape, a clear form attached to language. *I have a feeling that the speed of light is constant.*

When this dawning becomes a recognizable insight, we achieve the moment of clarity.

Psychologist Mihaly Csikszentmihalyi's famous studies on highly creative people observed that deep, quiet periods spent doing unrelated things often helped new ideas to surface within them: "Cognitive accounts of what happens during incubation assume . . . that some kind of information processing keeps going on in the mind even when we are not aware of it, even when we are asleep." Einstein's theory of relativity was occurring to him not in a flash but very slowly while he was making a sandwich, in the bath, during his morning walks, and most certainly while he was dreaming at night. In part 2 of this book, we will look more carefully at the experience of an insight dawning and the moment of clarity that follows. It's time to start getting people right.

PART TWO

Getting People Right

WHEN IT IS CLEAR that default thinking isn't working, people have a tendency to turn toward methods that aren't really methods at all. Before we discuss how a deeper investigation driven by the human sciences can solve business challenges, let's take a moment to debunk the most popular, but most misleading, strategic solutions on offer today.

The Big-Data Solution

The big-data solution—the tracking and number-crunching of vast amounts of consumer data, much of it available as digital traces— seduces us by promising a win in markets. Big data is alluring because it is presented in harmony with cutting-edge algorithms that promise to filter through vast amounts of information at a volume heretofore unprecedented. All of this is impressive, but the big-data solution places all of its emphasis on technology while downplaying the importance of the greatest computation machine: the human brain. After all, humans will, at some point, have to analyze the data, no matter how it is sliced and diced. Someone needs to have a perspective on what the algorithms deliver. It is this perspective—the moment of clarity—that requires time, deep thinking, and experience. Big data can't deliver on any of those things.

The "Steve Jobs" Solution

Surely you have heard this one over the last ten years. This solution argues convincingly that someone on your team should play the role of Steve Jobs. The intoxicating aspect is the notion that anyone can become Steve Jobs or think like him. The natural by-product of such claims is that the solution to your company's problem is to create the iPod or iPad of your industry. This silver bullet—so the solution tells us—will then save your company.

The Customization Solution

Your strategy becomes fixated on the idea that consumers want to have their products personalized. Whether this means that the consumers design the finishing touches on their product or that the experience of ownership is somehow customized to fit the consumers' lifestyles, the solution suggests that value comes from allowing the consumers to tinker with a series of superfluous features.

The Open Innovation Solution

Problems will be solved if innovation comes from outside the firm, the open innovation solution tells us. Outsource, crowdsource, share-source everything! If customers, partners, and entrepreneurs create your innovation through incentive efforts like contests and auctions, you will get better ideas and a wider variety of ways to win in the market.

The Social Media Solution

This solution promises that social media sites like Facebook and Twitter can transform a brand's relationship with its consumer base. Involving the consumers in the relationship—giving them the option to "like" or "retweet" gossip from their favorite brands—the solution tells us, will help to create more brand loyalty and generate the kinds of meaningful experiences that all brands hope to create with their customers.

While there may be truth and even inspiration from these solutions, none of them can form a long-term strategy for your company. None of them will provide you with a perspective on the market or do the messier work of revealing the changing phenomena at the core of your business. Take big data—obviously this is a very interesting opportunity: how do we capture and make sense of the data that comes from our customers' transactions on the internet? But big data is merely a tool for executing the bigger idea. You need a more profound understanding of what your products offer before you can filter through the noise of data analytics. Or think of Steve Jobs. He was an iconic leader, and Apple provides plenty of examples of inspiration. But the specificity of Jobs's vision—blending technology with the liberal arts—is not relevant for every industry. By focusing solely on another leader's success, we lose the ability to discern the game-changing opportunities for our own market successes. A leader can see things no one else can see, not by trying to imitate Jobs but by taking all his or her years of experience and practical knowledge and widening the lens on the leader's own industry landscape.

It's not easy to turn away from the reassurance of these ideas as long-term strategic solutions, but we all know they are limited. Only a deep investigation into our consumers' behavior will open up opportunities for innovation and future growth. Only an open-ended embrace of reality—life as it really is—will tell us what truly matters.

FOUR

The Human Sciences

I T WAS 2010 AND A major multinational electronics company was trying to understand the market for small digital cameras. In the past, it had held a majority market share in small, sleek, and relatively inexpensive cameras. These were the types of cameras that people used to pop in their weekend bag for vacation pictures or keep on the family mantle for photos of the kids at graduation or after the prom. Such cameras were never anything fancy, but they fulfilled their core purpose: they allowed people to take a small amount of good-quality photos that could then be printed out later for photo books and frames. These cameras served as documentation devices for a relatively limited amount of memorable occasions.

And then, suddenly, all of that changed.

"It's Not about the Camera"

First there was the camera phone and then the explosion of social networking sites and new photo-sharing capabilities. In a matter of only a few years, the company was completely in a fog. Did cameras even matter? What did kids want from their pictures? How could the company design new products when it didn't even understand the phenomenon of photography?

The company enlisted researchers to study teenagers' changing use of photography and snapshots across the United States. The researchers found that teenagers were uploading photographs in place of text—not just a few pictures but thousands and thousands of them. These photographs were not about documenting key events in the past; instead, they were enabling a dynamic conversation in the here and now. One researcher noted that in certain karaoke circles, one person was assigned to take a photograph every two minutes. These photographs were uploaded, shared, commented upon, and sometimes even deleted before the night had come to an end. The sheer amount of data—structured as a thread rather than as a coherent whole—was compromising the users' ability to retrieve or navigate information. Researchers noted that some kids were using social media postings to search for pictures instead of trying to find them in the camera's vast history of shots. Photography, once the realm of permanence, was now emblematic of the ephemeral. It was almost akin to a live performance.

All these changing practices required new capabilities from camera phones. Teenagers were looking for ways to process and sort through the thousands of images. They wanted a function that allowed them to mark certain photographs as keepsakes for sites like Instagram while sending the rest directly to a data garbage bin.

The company might have started its investigation with a question from default thinking: how do we recapture the market for cameras? But instead it chose to forgo any premature hypotheses. It simply spent time digging deeper into its consumers' behavior. What it found—digital photography is a form of live theater for the youth culture—was so much richer than something it might have come up with at a strategy session. Business implications followed organically: design cameras with easy tools for uploading directly to sites, and assume that because most photographs serve as a kind of fluid memory bank for users, make the search functions intuitive and allow them to quickly determine which photos will be permanent and which will be forgotten.

The executives at the company realized they could only ever really understand the camera within the context of its use. They recognized that it's not just about the camera; it's about the people.

Human sciences, or "soft sciences," are not based on the quantitative methods of the natural sciences. The study of people, cultures, relations, power, norms, and values requires different skills from those required in the study of molecules, crops, and stars. For those of us in the business world, there is little daily need to sit and ruminate on the workings of reality and how we interact with it. But what happens when the ever-increasing complexity of the business world delivers a challenge we don't understand: Is yoga a sport? How is television in the household changing? Why does everyone suddenly wear headphones? How is digital play growing? Why don't young people want to pay for media? In such moments of mystery, we need to look beyond numbers and spreadsheets and focus instead on experiences.

In this chapter, we offer a theoretical backdrop from the human sciences for solving these types of business challenges. The backdrop is by no means exhaustive, but it can serve as your guide while you begin to cultivate your own practice of open-ended inquiry. Note our use of the word *practice*. What we describe for you in the following chapters is less a set of hard and fast rules and more a musical score, a suggestive framework for artful interpretation. You'll find no five-step plan here, no seven secrets to such and such. What you will find is a theoretical scaffold for thinking differently about people as well as a method for applying the theory to your own business challenges. We call our method *sensemaking* because it describes the experience of connecting the dots amid a sea of confusing data. Through sensemaking, we arrive at moments of clarity. As your own practice grows deeper, you will likely develop your own names and heuristics. It will never be easy—no practice worth doing ever is—but your own version of sensemaking will start to feel intuitive the more you do it. Consider these chapters your primers. We will start with theory in this chapter and then move into more practical applications with business stories in chapters 5, 6, and 7. Let's begin by using the human-science lens to examine how people experience the world.

The Study of Experience

Phenomenology is the study of how people experience life. Although the word is rarely bandied about in a business context, phenomenology is the philosophical inspiration behind a method like sensemaking. It is the study of everything we feel in the world, everything that gives our lives meaning. Phenomenology can unlock the experience of driving a car or the sensation of being a mother. It is whether you see a Coke bottle and regard it with befuddlement, nostalgia, or disgust. In a pharma company, deductive reasoning can tell you how many salespeople met their quarter goals in 2010, but phenomenology will shed light on what, exactly, makes a good salesperson. In a *Fortune* 500 coffee company, management science can tell you how many premium cups of coffee the average American drinks in a day, but phenomenology will help you understand what constitutes the *experience* of really good coffee.

Properties versus Aspects

Any phenomenon—travel, sports, investing, entertainment, eating, or trust—can be analyzed using *property* data points from the hard sciences or experiential *aspects* from phenomenology. If biological gender (man or woman) is a property, then cultural gender (masculine or feminine) is the aspect. Science can help us determine if a person is a man or a woman, but how do we find out what it means to experience masculinity or femininity? What is being a man or woman *like*? Only the study of the phenomenon will help us understand that.

Things become meaningful when we start talking about aspects: a piece of fabric with three sewn colors becomes an American flag, a collection of molecules constituting gold becomes a wedding ring. Our experience in the world has to do with our investment in such objects and activities. How are kitchens, candy, soccer, or cell phones related to us? It is in this relatedness—this involvement in things—that objects have meaning. Although the brew might be exactly the same, a quick Styrofoam cup of coffee on the run is a vastly different experience from being served in fine china by a white-gloved waiter. The properties of the coffee are the same, but the aspects are not.

If all of this strikes you as decidedly unscientific—after all, how can you make a science out of the way things feel?—consider it in a different way. Phenomenology will not reveal the essence of something—say, a car or a restaurant—but rather will show the essence of our *relationship* to that thing. Not everything is important to us all the time. We stand in relationship to the things in our life, and phenomenology can show us which things matter most and when.

Another way to consider this argument is through the use of *correctness*, which is based on properties, and *truth*, based on aspects. If you ask Apple's iPhone application SIRI to tell you the difference between red and white onions, it will answer, "Six calories." While that answer is certainly correct, is it true? Within the frame of cooking, gardening, or even simply grocery shopping, does this answer tell us anything truthful?

Oh yes, you may say, but SIRI is a computational machine; such differences don't really apply to our marketing analysis or research and development, because we know what our customers like. Do you really, though? Beverage companies argue, for example, that sweetness drives liking. "When we put in more sugar," they tell us, "people like it more." Our response to that is, "Yes, that is correct. But is it *true*?" People will often say they like something in the moment, but what is their deeper relationship to it? Lots of people may like sweetness but they may, at the same time, experience cultural aversions to it, like fear or disgust. When you understand what drives the behavior of your consumers, you will reach a deeper insight that goes beyond the facts of correctness into the experience of truth.

Familiarity

Imagine an average day: we wake up, have breakfast, maybe drive to work or take the subway. All of this is familiar to us, unworthy of deeper examination. We think we know what it is to feel hungry or stuck in traffic or frustrated. But if we take any one thing and begin to look more closely, we find a subterranean world filled with surprising insights. Great philosophers have been directing our attention to this world for close to a hundred years. We can use words like *background* or *familiarity*, but other expressions, like *muscle memory*, *common sense*, *natural behavior*, and *what one does* all express a similar notion. The radical idea is that most of our life is not steered by thinking at all, but is guided rather by our familiarity—our act of *being*—in the world. We are not conscious of the concept of a kitchen knife or a washing machine or a lawn mower. We simply use them. They withdraw from our attention and turn into background the more involved we are. And we do this so deftly, so fluidly, that in most circumstances, our own behavior is invisible to us. Part 1 endeavored to show how our own business culture of default thinking exists all around us—filled with assumptions so familiar to us that we can no longer even discern them. Famed German film director Wim Wenders named one of his most acclaimed movies after this experience of familiarity: *In weiter Ferne, so nah!* (*Faraway, So Close*). This *faraway, so close* familiarity makes up phenomenology, or everything we experience in the world.

Take the very familiar concept of money. Instead of examining money's properties—cellulose with ink printed on it—try to examine its aspects. Money is a shared language for value. Most of us prefer more rather than less. Many of us are afraid of it. Others find it arousing, while certain cultures refuse to even speak of it out loud. When designing accounts for their customers, banks typically give people with more money more access to it. In a banker's world, it is vital for top clients to have full transparency with their account. But if you look more closely at how wealthy people *feel* about their money—how they experience having or spending money—a banker's world may not be the most appropriate mind-set for designing an account. After all, most people with money don't want to see it every day. They want to be assured that it is safe, but they don't have any interest in counting it the way bankers do. For this reason, bankers almost inevitably do better when they deconstruct their own culture before imposing it directly on the various cultures of their customers.

The slogan of phenomenology is "to the things themselves." The idea is to study the thing itself—be it a work of literature, death, the family, a car, or the hospital—without preconceived notions or reductionist theories or dogma imposed on it. This is the only way to achieve an insight into something both *faraway* and *so close*.

How to Begin the Study of Experiences

Any open-ended method like sensemaking is primarily built around this study of experiences. You don't need to know doctrines of philosophy—sometimes it is better if you don't—nor do you have to memorize Western civilization's greatest hits. Think of this as a DIY philosophy. Start by looking at the complexity and beauty of the world. Try to describe what you are experiencing and how you are experiencing it. How did you—really—go from the experience of not knowing to making a decision? How did you—honestly—make choices about this year's budget? When did you—truly—decide the numbers for the new product launch? A reasonable guess is that most of these decisions were made not in an entirely rational way, but on a gut-instinct level. What did you *feel*? This is where the study of experience begins: with the individual experience. It is not, however, a license to opine or navel-gaze. The subjective experience is only the beginning. We use it to think about how to gather the best data to uncover the patterns occurring in a market as a whole. Phenomenology is interested not in the extraordinary, but in the ordinary and commonplace for all (or most) of us. In this way, it isn't about the R^2 statistic or the significant sample size. In fact, a useful study of experiences would need to look at only a decent amount of people and their situations. These experiences should be collected and understood if a business is going to fully see the patterns of behavior that all people share.

If we can say anything about the study of experience, it is this: get out of the office and away from the spreadsheets. Don't start your inquiry with the theoretical. Only experience stripped of hypothesis will reveal the rich reality of humanity. We break down the study of human experience into three building blocks:

1. A fairly sophisticated *outlook* on what it means to be a human being and on life in its totality

2. Human-science theories and tools such as ethnography, thick description, an understanding of worlds, and double loop

3. The methodology of *abductive reasoning*

A Sophisticated Outlook on Human Experience

After the publication of her first books, Alice Munro—a revered Canadian fiction writer and winner of the 2013 Nobel Prize for Literature—started receiving fan letters from other writers. These letters were requesting what Munro later described as "brass tacks" information about the writing life. "Is it necessary to work on a computer? Have an agent? Associate with other writers?" Really, of course, the writers were asking Munro how she managed to capture the essence of life in language. How does one describe all of the mystery, heartbreak, joy, and grace that go into our own human existence? How does one describe "life"?

Munro might have responded to these letters with facts, or properties. She might have told writers exactly when she did her writing (in between other household responsibilities), where she did her writing (at the table and then, later, at an old desk), and what piece of equipment she used to make these scribblings appear permanently on paper (a pen, most often). But these details—the *hard science* of her accumulated writing experience—struck her as absurd.

> It assumes that I am a person of brisk intelligence, exercising steady control on a number of fronts. [That] I make advantageous judgments concerning computers and themes, I chart a course which is called a career and expect to make progress in it.

Munro was never able to answer these letters with "brass tacks" information. In one of her stories, however, her imagined character describes the futility of attempting to capture the facts of life as it is lived:

> I would try to make lists. A list of all the stores and businesses going up and down Main Street and who owned them, a list of family names, names on the tombstones in the cemetery and any inscriptions underneath . . . The hope of accuracy we bring to such tasks is crazy, heartbreaking. And no list could ever hold what I wanted, for what I wanted was every last thing, every layer of speech and thought, stroke of light on bark or walls, every smell, pothole, pain, crack, delusion, held still and held together—radiant, everlasting.

We all know that life is complex: mysterious, by turns banal, and then, in moments, touched by transcendence. Humans live in a reality that is textured, nuanced, complicated, filled with *every last thing.* Try, like Alice Munro, to make a list of everything that you know in your embodied experience of the world. Experienced soldiers in Iraq describe the sensation of "feeling" the booby traps in their bodies upon getting near to these devices. Seasoned firefighters can intuit when the floor is going to collapse beneath them. George Soros, veritable emperor in the world of investing and high finance, knows that something is not right in the markets when the pain in his back acts up. Famed dancer and choreographer Twyla Tharp described the experience of watching her dancer Rose Marie Wright teach a dance that Wright learned thirty some years ago to a group of new dancers in the company: "If she demonstrates the dance without thinking about it, she will re-create each step and gesture perfectly on the spot the first time, as though she were a medium in a trance. That's muscle memory. Automatic. Precise. A little scary. The second time through, however, or trying to explain the steps and patterns to the dancers, she will hesitate, second-guess herself, question her muscles, and forget. That's because she is thinking about it, using language to interpret something she knows nonverbally. Her memory of movement doesn't need to be accessed through conscious effort."

The best of life—the richest existential layers—are deeply encoded within such details. The famous Japanese woodworker, Toshio Odate, told his students during one of his many master sessions, "You enjoy chisels, you enjoy planes, you enjoy the feeling of this organic material. You have to train your body to sensitivity. That's the key. Then you learn how to sharpen chisels, you feel the vibration. You can feel the resistance of many different types of wood." Odate explained that about a third of woodworking could be learned intellectually, by reading. The majority of it had to come from daily repetition: hands on the wood, the smells, the different blades, and even the painful cuts in the skin.

In the best of his music, famed trumpeter Miles Davis is described as playing not what is on the page but "the ghost note," interpolating musical and historical influences with the nuances of every sound coming out of his trumpet. Terence Blanchard, contemporary trumpeter and devotee of Davis, explained, "When Miles Davis played a simple phrase, sometimes that expressed something with more elegance and beauty than any very technically accomplished phrase could say." Davis himself put it simply: "Don't play what's there; play what's not there."

As the great philosophers of the twentieth century argue, if your outlook on life does not include this level of depth and richness—this embodied knowledge—you will never really understand people's behavior. Our argument directly contradicts the prevailing approach of the current business culture: default thinking. If we were to create a philosophical death match to illustrate our point, we would pair René Descartes—father of rational thinking, or minds *detached* from the world—against Martin Heidegger, the philosopher who argued that human beings are at their best when deeply *embedded* in the world.

Not every decision people make is rational and diligent. They buy things they don't need, do things that are a waste of time, and sometimes hold sacred their various decisions made on a whim. This is why religion, magic, love, music, art, beauty, literature, and national parks don't make any sense in a rational universe. Over the last millennia, this deep divide between rational thought and real life has led philosophers to divide human beings into strange sets of two: body and spirit, subject and object, sense and sensibility.

To understand this divide, we must go all the way back to Plato and his deep interest in theory and mathematics. His whole philosophy is predicated on the idea that things (including us) are at their best when they are universal and devoid of any particularities. The horses that run around in the field aren't as perfect as the *idea* of a horse; a vase on the table is not as perfect as the *idea* of a vase. Plato's philosophy led to the notions we all live by every day in modern society: human beings are, above all, *thinking* things; we strive for perfection in rational thought; the cleanliness of theory is better than the particular things around us; and we are subjects giving meaning to objects in the world. According to Plato, we have a perfect map of the world in our minds, and we use it to make sense of everything around us. Descartes was the philosopher who most powerfully described this vision of us as rational thinking beings: minds floating outside the world. He conceived of us as seeing the world through a window of ideas rather than being directly involved in it. In Descartes's view, we humans are and should be autonomous agents making rational decisions. He believed that we have full access to our minds and, therefore, know what we want. Following that argument, we shouldn't take tradition, moods, or emotions into account, but rather should maintain a cold, distant relationship with what is around us.

When we argue for a conception of human experience that differs from conventional business perspectives, we are arguing for the phenomenological tradition led, primarily, by Martin Heidegger, author of the groundbreaking masterpiece written in 1927, *Being and Time*. Heidegger wrote that we are at our best not when we are sitting, detached and thinking, but when we are deeply involved in the world—when we forget about where we are and engage in activities that we can master. Heidegger is not saying that we never think. He is the first to agree that science exists because of our ability to think. But he argues that most people are so embedded in their daily activities that they don't need to think. When a trained chef is making a soufflé, he or she does not step back and think about the whisk and the bowl. The chef is deeply and practically involved in the world. Heidegger said that rather than being thinking things, we are "beings in the world." In his work, he dismantles over two thousand years' worth of philosophical tradition, blurring the distinctions between rational and irrational, subject and object. In his new tradition of philosophy, phenomena like love, trust, hatred, and beauty are examined through our experience of them in our everyday lives.

Human-Science Theories and Tools

Human science employs numerous techniques to recognize and describe the experiences that all people have. Let's look at some of the most important tools that businesses can use to understand both their own customers and the broader market.

Ethnography

Consider the following chronology in Bruno Latour's ethnographic description of a modern American workplace:

> *5 mins.* John enters and goes into his office. He says something very quickly about having made a bad mistake. He had sent the review of a paper. . . . The rest of the sentence is inaudible.
>
> *5 mins. 30 secs.* Barbara enters. She asks Spencer what kind of solvent to put on the column. Spencer answers from his office. Barbara leaves and goes to the bench.
>
> *5 mins. 35 secs.* Jane comes in and asks Spencer: "When you prepare for I.V. with morphine, is it in saline or in water?" Spencer, apparently writing at his desk, answers from his office. Jane leaves.
>
> *6 mins. 15 secs.* Wilson enters and looks into a number of offices, trying to gather people together for a staff meeting. He receives vague promises. "It's a question of four thousand bucks which has to be resolved in the next two minutes, at most." He leaves for the lobby.
>
> *6 mins. 20 secs.* Bill comes from the chemistry section and gives Spencer a thin vial: "Here are your two hundred micrograms, remember to put this code number on the book," and he points to the label. He leaves the room.
>
> Long silence. The library is empty. Some write in their offices, some work by windows in the brightly lit bench space. The staccato noise of typewriting can be heard from the lobby.
>
> *9 mins.* Julius comes in eating an apple and perusing a copy of *Nature*.
>
> *9 mins. 10 secs.* Julie comes in from the chemistry section, sits down on the table, unfolds the computer sheets she

was carrying, and begins to fill in a sheet of paper. Spencer emerges from his office, looks over her shoulder and says: "hmm, looks nice." He then disappears into John's office with a few pages of draft.

9 mins. 20 secs. A secretary comes in from the lobby and places a newly typed draft on John's desk. She and John briefly exchange remarks about deadlines.

9 mins. 30 secs. Immediately following her, Rose, the inventory assistant, arrives to tell John that a device he wants to buy will cost three hundred dollars. They talk in John's office and laugh. She leaves.

Silence again.

10 mins. John screams from his office: "Hey Spencer, do you know of any clinical group reporting production of SS in tumor cells?" Spencer yells back from his office: "I read that in the abstracts of the Asilomar conference, it was presented as a well-known fact." John: "What was the evidence for that?" Spencer: "Well, they got an increase in . . . and concluded it was due to SS. Maybe, I'm not sure they directly tested biological activities, I'm not sure." John: "Why don't you try it on next Monday's bioassay?"

10 mins. 55 secs. Bill and Mary come in suddenly. They are at the end of a discussion. "I don't believe this paper," says Bill. "No, it's so badly written. You see, it must have been written by an M.D." They look at Spencer and laugh.

Making observations without presupposing a model is a mental challenge. What strange tribe is this? How do they communicate? What do they value? Eventually, without more of a context, we begin to wiggle and twitch internally. "I need to understand what is happening!" we think to ourselves. Most of us long to leave the realm of doubt and rest easily again in confident knowledge and understanding. "They are businesspeople!" "No, they are professors at a university." "Ah! I get it! They are research scientists!"

Ethnography—the process of observing, documenting, and then analyzing behavior—is one of the main data collection techniques for human sciences. Used in everything from anthropology and sociology to history and philosophy, ethnography is an imperative focus for analyzing phenomena. The technique emerged in the nineteenth century, when the study of society exploded through the scholarship of thinkers like Karl Marx and Emile Durkheim. It wasn't until 1922, however, with the work of Polish anthropologist Bronisław Kasper Malinowski, that the professional practice of *participatory observation* was defined and distinguished from the grab bag of techniques used by journalists, missionaries, and travelers.

Malinowski is widely considered the most skilled anthropologist in the history of the discipline. The majority of his research comes from his time spent in Papua New Guinea, particularly during World War I, when he became stranded on the Trobriand Islands, unable to return to Europe from the British-controlled region because he was a Pole from Austria-Hungary. Malinowski spent his period of exile as a participant-observer in the Kula tribe, ultimately turning his analyses into the ethnographic masterpiece, *Argonauts of the Western Pacific.* In this book, he lays out the foundation for the anthropologist's role as a scientific analyst versus a mere describer: "The integration of all the details observed, the achievement of a sociological synthesis of all the various, relevant symptoms, is the task of the Ethnographer . . . The Ethnographer has to construct the picture of the big institution, very much as the physicist constructs his theory from the experimental data, which always have been within reach of everybody, but needed a consistent interpretation."

Descriptive observation came first, followed by an educated guess at an analytical interpretation. Ethnography, using methods like participatory observation, was a radical, open-ended approach to understanding other cultures. It involved immersing oneself in the object of study rather than focusing on proving or disproving a hypothesis. With its emphasis on immersion, ethnography stands in contrast to other research techniques that aim to help businesses understand human experience, such as the use of desk-based market research and focus groups. While conventional forms of market research can play an important role in creating business strategies, market research is not the same thing as ethnography; nor does it deliver the same richly textured results. As we will discuss in later chapters, both LEGO and Coloplast had undertaken significant market research programs before turning to sensemaking and ethnography as their main data collection method.

Ethnography is best understood, like everything in the human sciences, within a context. Say your business needs to gain insight into the growing middle class in China. You might turn to properties— upward mobility will move hundreds of millions of households from poverty to prosperity in the next decade. But what do those numbers mean for an individual's experience of upward mobility? What is it like to pack up your life and move from a rural to an urban setting? How do you settle in? What is important? Is it confusing? Great? Both? An ethnographic perspective can offer up the aspects—or the experience—of such a sweeping sociological change. By looking at one ethnographer's intimate interaction with one middle-class Chinese man, we can gain far greater insight into the phenomenon than we ever could poring over reams and reams of consumer data.

Notes from the Field: What Does an Ethnographic
Insight Look Like?

Eliot Salandy Brown, a researcher for ReD Associates, conducted an ethnographic study to get a glimpse of everyday life for a Chinese family. Here is part of his story:

> It was on my fourth attempt to find out what Wei Bao thought of the changes tearing through his neighborhood that I realized I wasn't going to get an answer. Not like this. The ethnography had started well. After I took off my shoes and presented a small gift of Danish biscuits, Wei Bao welcomed me into his sparsely furnished living room. Minutes later, sipping tiny thimbles of rich, earthy 'Pu'er tea his bright eyes darting between me and his wife, Wei Bao excitedly told the story of the day he was finally promoted to chief engineer at a small mine 20 kilometers west of Fuzhou.
>
> "It was my discipline that made the difference," he explained, his wife nodding knowingly next to him. "I'm a predictable man, and my bosses always knew they could depend on me to be steady."
>
> It was on the day of that promotion 30 years ago that Wei Bao was given the apartment we sat in now. Constructed in the early 1970s, the apartment was more or less identical to the 250 others surrounding it. Peering past his washing hanging on the balcony, I could make out men of Wei Bao's age playing mah-jongg in the dusty courtyard, the clatter of the plastic pieces drifting up in the still autumn air.
>
> "We are proud to live here because it means you have been recognized by the government. It is an honor, in a way." An hour earlier, walking up the dim stairwell with its discolored concrete and broken lights, I would not have guessed at the symbolic

value of this address. But on reflection, I realized it was not only the condition of the building that had led me to assume that this was a rather standard piece of real estate. It was the contrast with what surrounded it. Wei Bao's worn-out housing complex now stands like a solitary gray pebble in an otherwise shimmering pool of blue glass. Fueled by Taiwanese investment, towering apartment complexes, neon-fronted restaurants, high-ceilinged European car dealerships, and mobile-phone shops have invaded Wei Bao's neighborhood, bringing with them a new generation of Chinese consumers who shop for leisure, not just out of necessity, and like coffee as much as tea.

And what I now wanted to understand was how Wei Bao felt about all this. Was this progress or destruction? What was his common ground with the younger generations? Was Fuzhou westernizing or giving birth to a whole new interpretation of China? How did all of this make him feel about China's future trajectory?

Nothing. Four attempts to get subjective perspectives had gotten me four pages of objective statistics. Wei Bao used his almost encyclopedic knowledge of population growth, urban migration rates, investment sources, and bank-loan rates to studiously avoid giving me the faintest idea of how he felt. And I was starting to panic. I get paid to find out what people feel, fear, regret, admire, desire, and I was about to go home with nothing but data.

As though perceiving my horrific visions of returning to my bosses without knowing anything more interesting than his tea preferences ('Pu'er every time), Wei Bao made a suggestion. "Why don't we go and see my new apartment?"

Five minutes later he was confidently whisking me through traffic on the back of his electric scooter, clearly enjoying the challenge presented by Fuzhou's unpredictable traffic, and 10 minutes later we stood with our heads as far back as they would go, staring up at a sparkling 49-story apartment building cutting into the low gray sky.

"It's an investment together with my son. He's having his first child soon, and this is where they will live. Come, let me show you around." The "steady," quiet man I had met in his government apartment disappeared as Wei Bao sprang around the unfinished apartment explaining where the dishwasher, washing machine, microwave, and TV ("of course, plasma") would sit. He showed me the designs he'd been working on for the glass-and-steel kitchen, the recessed lighting, and his proudest contribution—the walk-in shower. And on his balcony, overlooking dozens of new buildings in which thousands of new Chinese dreams just like his were being constructed, Wei Bao finally opened up.

"I often stand here and think about how China has progressed. I imagine the life my grandson will have and compare it with mine—there's no doubt things are better. Young people have an energy now that we didn't have. It's like they have a light on inside them that we had to switch off and aren't brave enough to switch on again."

I ask him what it was about his life that was difficult, and after a long gaze out over the buildings he says, "It was restrictive. Limited. My son thinks he can be who he wants to be, professionally and as a person, and that is a very fortunate situation."

Wei Bao tells me that the Chinese way isn't always best and it's good to be inspired by what other countries do. That he would like to travel and see the world, especially Italy. That perhaps his old apartment building and the men playing mah-jongg will one day disappear, and that's not such a shame.

As we left the apartment after three hours on the balcony, I realized what had allowed this quiet man to begin telling me what he really thought and felt. The answer was simple—we had moved to a social and physical context in which it was appropriate. Sitting with his faithful wife by his side, in the home given to him by the government, surrounded by proud artifacts from his younger days, it was not an option for Wei Bao to speak his mind. His wife would have lost face, he would have been indirectly criticizing his peers in the surrounding apartments, he would have seemed ungrateful, and he would have made any Chinese guest very uncomfortable.

I have taken Wei Bao's lesson with me, and when I'm in China now I always present people with a range of social and physical contexts that allow the various facets of their personality and perspectives to be expressed and explored. For this lesson I am very grateful to Wei Bao. Indeed, to thank him for such an enlightening day, I invited Wei Bao to dinner.

"Where would you like to go?" I asked him. "There's that famous Chinese restaurant near your bus stop."

"No," he replied. "You see that one over there on the corner? They do the best cheeseburger and fries in all of Fuzhou."

Thick Description

The ethnographer's insights into Wei Bao's perspective give us an example of what the American anthropologist Clifford Geertz famously describes as *thick description*. Geertz spent the lion's share of his academic career writing about the nuances of culturally complex gestures, the *thickness* that adds depth to life. Take the wink. The computer might classify it as a twitch of the eye lasting for a millisecond, but we all know that a wink can mean so much more. This tiny movement has the ability to say, "Let's leave together," "You're an idiot," "I'm not serious," and so many other more ineffable desires.

To illustrate the importance of thick description to any complex understanding of human behavior, we can take something as culturally familiar as an Adele song. Try this thought exercise: think of Adele as thick and then thin.

At the 2012 Grammys, the British singer Adele took home six awards for her wildly popular album *21*. Part of the music industry's fever-pitch adoration of Adele has to do with her ability to create music that feels authentic, personal, intimate, and individualized—we sympathize with her emotions as if they're our own. So much so that a recent *Saturday Night Live* skit portrays an office worker putting on Adele's song "Someone Like You" for a good cry, only to have the entire office gather around her for a grand collective sob session.

The *Wall Street Journal* recently responded to this phenomenon by asking, "What is it about Adele's music that is so good at making us cry?" To answer this, they turned to empirical studies of musical triggers of emotional responses, measured by physiological changes such as spikes in heart rate, the appearance of goose bumps, or sweating. For example, as reported in the *Wall Street Journal*:

> Chill-provoking passages . . . shared at least four features.
> They began softly and then suddenly became loud. They
> included an abrupt entrance of a new "voice," either a new
> instrument or harmony. And they often involved an expansion
> of the frequencies played. In one passage from Mozart's Piano

Concerto No. 23 (K. 488), for instance, the violins jump up one octave to echo the melody. Finally, all the passages contained unexpected deviations in the melody or the harmony. Music is most likely to tingle the spine, in short, when it includes surprises in volume, timbre and harmonic pattern.

While surely the neuroscience behind the analysis is more nuanced, presenting the emotional power of music in this way seems impoverished. It takes something magical and reduces it to the appearance of this or that stylistic device. But it misses another important point: cultural context influences which products we perceive as emotionally resonant and how our emotional reaction plays itself out. This is because cultural context affects our relationship to our own emotions—how we think about them and how we experience them. In other words, what makes a song emotionally evocative is partly contingent on time and place.

The emotions these stylistic devices trigger become commodities similar to others that we consume regularly. We eat a candy bar when we feel like we deserve a treat; we listen to Adele when we feel blue. In this way, the relationship between emotions and cultural products is commoditized.

So because we have grown up in the particular context that the culture industry has produced, we know that Adele is the kind of music we should listen to when we feel sad. This relationship between emotions and pop culture pieces (how they're thought about and experienced) is a unique product of our contemporary culture industry. This way of thinking about the issue doesn't delegitimize the emotional response of someone who finds Adele's song moving. It does, however, imply that the emotional dynamic underneath the goose bumps is wrapped up in a whole different set of culturally conditioned baggage than, say, those experienced by the first audience members who heard Bach's famous *Ciaccona.*

So what can businesses learn from all of this? Though the natural sciences can scientifically measure heart rates and goose bumps, the measuring machines are giving us a thin description of properties and no insights into aspects. There are millions of ways to experience goose bumps; each way is thick with meaning.

Understanding Worlds

Any attempt to accurately study thick description needs to examine how the background—the system of various worlds—is structured. What kind of invisible scaffolding is present in our everyday lives dictating our actions and supporting our beliefs? This idea was introduced in chapter 2 through Pierre Bourdieu's concept of habitus. But it can be explored in more depth through the human-science lens.

In our everyday language, we talk about the business world, the theater world, or the world of high finance. These are names for sets of equipment, practices, and words that connect and become a system, or a *world.* If you want to work in the theater world, it is helpful to have equipment like tickets, a stage, critics, and actors making up the world. It would be impossible to be, say, a playwright, without a preexisting understanding of what is meaningful in the world of theater. When a politician doesn't understand the rules of the world of politics, for example, he or she is immediately labeled politically tone-deaf. Only insiders to the world of saltwater fly-fishing will know what a grand slam is, when to be quiet, and how to tip a guide. And jazz insiders know when to clap and what to order at the bar. In this way, we all belong to a series of worlds that run on their own logic and set their own rules. When someone from the outside enters—an ethnographer, for example—he or she has an opportunity to see the familiar in the strange, and the strange in the familiar.

As social animals, we learn the rules of our worlds fast and adapt to them collectively, just as instruments in a symphonic orchestra are tuned together before the concert begins. *Attunement*—getting in sync with a world or learning its rules—is a key social skill that we all have, one we need if we are to switch fluidly between worlds. We all know the phenomenon of entering a party in a grumpy mood. If the party is great, our mood soon dissipates and we, too, are in sync with that great feeling.

An understanding of worlds necessitates an understanding of social norms, that is, the customs and practices that all (or most) of us follow without ever consciously thinking about it. All the unspoken rules that we follow every day—present but invisible— can be investigated through phenomenology. If an American soda brand wants to launch its product lines in China, the brand would find it extraordinarily helpful to understand how a person behaves around mealtime or whenever soda is consumed. A vodka manufacturer would profit from understanding what someone does around a mixing and cocktail culture. And a car company would make fewer mistakes if only it understood how a person buys a car. When the executives at the athletic shoe company were befuddled by the question "Is yoga a sport?" much of their confusion was a result of their social norms. A person simply did not do sport without competition. This normative behavior was adhered to so strongly within the company culture that it was next to impossible for the executives to conceive of an alternative culture.

All these examples underscore that despite what we may think, we are not individuals. We are, all of us, situated in a context. If we are to understand human behavior, then we must understand context, an argument for the holistic versus the atomized. Once we embrace the importance of context, it becomes impossible to strip people and objects away from their embedded circumstances.

At the opening of Jamie Uys's 1981 comedy *The Gods Must Be Crazy*, for example, a Coke bottle drops from the sky into a tribe of Kalahari Bushmen. It is a mysterious object of wonder—a gift from the gods, surely—and the people try to find the best use for it. Is it a weapon? A storage tube? A decoration? At the end of the movie, even while fighting over who gets to keep it, the aura of the Coke bottle never reveals itself. Its very "Cokeness" is meaningless out of context.

We in the West, of course, have an entirely different relationship with the Coke bottle. Whether we look at the bottle and think about the shape of a woman's body or we taste the liquid and get transported back to our childhood, Coke is more than just an object. As discussed earlier, the Coke bottle functions within an entire series of relational worlds, what we might call *chains of meaning*. We can even extend this idea further by saying that all tools—the stuff that surrounds us—are organized into chains of meaning, and the meaning is frequently revealed by the phrase *in order to*. A hammer is only a hammer when it is used in order to a build a frame in order to create a shelter in order to provide a home in order to make the homeowner feel secure. I drink Coke in order to stay awake in order to be productive in order to be successful in order to be loved. And so on.

Because our understanding of the world is based entirely on context, we can only ever truly understand our tools—our mobile phones, our coffee, our cars—when these objects break down. We can only understand what it means to be online when, suddenly, we are unable to get online. Our phones only make sense to us when someone takes them away. A line for a coffee cart outside our office only becomes clear to us when we are from a culture that does not stand in line for coffee. Things withdrawn from our understanding, from our mere consideration, come to the fore when they are disconnected from their chains of meaning. Only through this disconnection do we gain true understanding about our worlds.

Double Loop

The big difference between studying human beings and studying an object in the natural world—say, a leaf—is that leaves don't become self-conscious. When you fill out a questionnaire about your perception of beer brands, for example, how accurately do you report your behavior? Are you attempting to make a certain impression on your surveyors? Are you changing your behavior according to what you deem appropriate or inappropriate? And can you actually answer the questions with any kind of certainty in the first place? And then, of course, there is the person observing you—collecting the survey or asking you the question or even sitting across the table from you over coffee. He or she can't avoid filtering your behavior through his or her own mental models of the world.

Even social scientists like anthropologists behave according to an invisible system of rules. For this very reason, they must be vigilant about keeping their own cultural biases in check. This is the greatest challenge of ethnography: as the line between subject and object blurs—and with it, the promise of an objective reality—the ethnographer must always be observing his or her own assumptions while also analyzing those of the culture. This phenomenon—what we call *double loop*—is a conundrum that all social scientists grapple with. In the natural sciences, it is possible to observe phenomena objectively—the study of quarks or the size of a star—but the human sciences require the point of view of the human scientist. When a person is observing human behavior, there is no view from nowhere; it is necessary to acknowledge and assess one's own biases. This is not always an easy or straightforward task, but what is the alternative? As we have seen, to give up on an interpretation of phenomena—choosing instead to look at one-dimensional data in the form of properties—is to give up on 99 percent of life as it is really lived.

The best human scientists attempt to understand their own values and biases just as they are studying the values and biases of another culture. They bring themselves to the endeavor and the big-picture insights they create—or *construct*, to use Malinowski's terminology—engaging both the analytical mind and aesthetic sensibilities. The moment of clarity arrives through the methodology of abductive reasoning.

Abductive Reasoning

How do we make discoveries? How do we observe phenomena, and what will prejudice or change the way we observe things? Is it right to start with a set of ideas rather than start from scratch and see where our work leads us? In which situations is it okay to start with a hypothesis and test it? In which situations is it better not to have any preconceived notions at all? These are all different ways of reasoning through a problem: a concern at the center of a centuries-old debate about the scientific method. In the late 1800s, American philosopher and logician Charles Sanders Peirce became famous for defining the three kinds of reasoning used to solve problems—abduction, induction, and deduction—each appropriate for different levels of certainty.

Peirce contended that only abductive reasoning—starting with observation and then moving next to possible hypotheses—was capable of generating new ideas. Deduction effectively evolved a hypothesis but was unable to incorporate new information. And the problem with induction, Peirce argued, was that the analysis was never exhaustive—one could always find more ways of looking at something. As we argued in chapter 2, when you reason inductively, you have limited yourself to one set of beliefs—all well and good for certain types of problems with set knowns and unknowns—but no longer useful for problems involving culture and behavior. Abduction, Peirce described in his 1903 Harvard "Lectures on Pragmatism," was both more compelling and more problematic: "The abductive suggestion comes to us like a flash but it is not a flash available to all. It is an act of insight, although of extremely fallible insight. It is true that the different elements of the hypothesis were in our minds before; but it is the idea of putting together what we had never before dreamed of putting together, which flashes the new suggestion before our contemplation."

For Peirce, abduction was about looking for answers. While the previous few hundred years had been about the development of science and the belief that the industrial age could conquer anything, Peirce, in his lecture "First Rule of Logic" (1899), questioned what we thought we knew. "Do not block the way of inquiry," he said, putting forth four offenses that we commit when we reason:

1. We make an absolute assertion that we're right.

2. We believe that something isn't knowable, because we don't have the techniques or technologies to figure it out.

3. We insist that some element of science is utterly inexplicable and unknowable.

4. We believe that some law or truth is in its final and perfect state.

Peirce rejected the notion that any theory was "true" while maintaining that it could be "near true." In other words, he believed there was always room for improvement and endless potential for new "truths" to emerge.

It's easy to see why scientists would dismiss the idea that you cannot come to the end of something—that "facts" are not necessarily conclusive. But one of Peirce's most significant contributions was to distinguish between the act of asking a question and the act of making a judgment, which we experience as doubt and belief, respectively: "Doubt is an uneasy and dissatisfied state from which we struggle to free ourselves and pass into the state of belief; while the latter is a calm and satisfactory state which we do not wish to avoid, or to change to a belief in anything else."

Why is it so difficult for us to change our minds? Peirce argued that our discomfort with doubt—not a lack of knowledge—leads us to hold fast to outdated and sometimes downright foolish ideas. Our blind faith makes us appear like an ostrich burying its head in the sand to hide from the danger while, at the same time, denying the existence of anything dangerous. Humans, like ostriches, tend to avoid dealing with anything that might change their core beliefs. If this requires turning a blind eye to mounting evidence or shutting out a voice of reason, so be it.

For better or for worse, abductive reasoning is *uncomfortable*. But it is only through such problem solving that we can achieve the moment of clarity, the foundation of genuine creativity.

As you will see in the business stories to follow, executive leaders felt their creative insight before they thought it. They experienced a dawning directly followed by the moment of clarity. Their insights were not the result of number-crunching on the spreadsheets or better slides in the deck. Every key insight came out of a deep reflective process involving a visceral connection with the data.

In these forthcoming chapters, we leave theory behind and look at how a method like sensemaking applies to real business challenges. To help guide us, we break down sensemaking into five phases:

1. Frame the problem as a phenomenon.

2. Collect the data.

3. Look for patterns.

4. Create the key insights.

5. Build the business impact.

The moment of clarity is different for every business challenge. In the chapters that follow, we'll discuss how different companies have used these methods to find their own moments of clarity and how their experiences can serve as a guide for your efforts. For example, the toymaker LEGO Group needed to set a long-term direction—the quintessential corporate turnaround story—so it experienced several moments of clarity, all dismantling assumptions the company had long held about the way children play. The process that Coloplast, a medical products manufacturer, used, by contrast, focused on product design in a single business within the corporation. For this company, sensemaking culminated in one dramatic moment of clarity that changed its entire value proposition. And for companies like Adidas and Intel, a nonlinear process of problem solving predicated on key insights is driving the entire corporate strategy into the future.

FIVE

The Turnaround

LEGO

IT'S A DREARY LATE FALL day in Billund, Denmark. In a town of around six thousand people and a handful of stoplights, one would expect a small airport with a coffee cart and a single runway. Instead, Billund is the second-largest airport in Denmark, bustling with hundreds of international flights coming in and out every day. The town wastes no time in communicating its chief benefactor and honorary citizen; in fact, the smiling, square head of the iconic yellow man greets you at every turn. Billund is home to the LEGO Group, one of the largest and most respected toy companies in the world.

At the company headquarters, giant red, yellow, and blue bricks are visible through the gloomy fog. The reception desk is, you guessed it, an enormous brick broken in half. And a life-size yellow LEGO man holds a computer welcome screen at the entrance. Considering the pride behind the LEGO brand on display across the campus, it is hard to imagine that only eight years ago, the iconic brick was lying on its deathbed. LEGO has undergone an astounding turnaround since 2004, driven, in part, by its commitment to a sensemaking practice.

In the 1930s, Danish carpenter Ole Kirk Christiansen started making tiny versions of his work projects—toy furniture and games. In 1947, he moved from wood to plastic, ultimately creating a full product line of toys. He named his company LEGO from the Danish *leg godt*, or "play well," and, in 1958, his company patented its now-famous stud-and-tube coupling system, or the click-fit. An iconic children's toy was born. The core patent remains unchanged even now, more than fifty years later.

But after decades of growth and innovation—in 2000, the company was the fifth-largest toy maker in the world—LEGO hit a major slump. In January 2004, it announced a huge deficit. It was, by its own accounts, bleeding cash to the tune of $1 million a day. Owner and CEO Kjeld Kirk Kristiansen, grandson of founder Ole Kirk Christiansen, was at the helm of a strategy to turn the company around. He stepped down and appointed Jørgen Vig Knudstorp, a former McKinsey consultant, as new CEO of the company.

Somehow, the company honored with the Best Toy of the Century award *twice* had completely lost touch with its core consumers. How did it happen? And how did LEGO come out of the fog and solve its own mystery?

"Back to the Brick"

The answers are revealed in LEGO's commitment to an open-ended inquiry. The company used theories from the human sciences and applied them to the sensemaking method, exploring the behavior of its customers:

Sensemaking: Five Phases

1. Frame the problem as a phenomenon.

2. Collect the data.

3. Look for patterns.

4. Create the key insights.

5. Build the business impact.

Phase 1: Frame the Problem as a Phenomenon

For LEGO, framing the problem as a phenomenon meant reframing the question from "What toys do kids want?" to "What is the role of play?"

If you ran into Paal Smith-Meyer on the street, you might mistake him for a grad student. In his late thirties and dressed in an unzipped hoodie with a dusting of scruff on his chin, he could not appear more casual. But Smith-Meyer, currently head of the new business group, is one of several design powerhouses at the helm of LEGO's new strategy.

He started at the company in 1999 as a designer. "To me," he explained, "LEGO was all about the brick. So you can imagine my surprise when I showed up in the early aughts and there was not much interest in it. It was all about the LEGO *brand*."

The company was leveraging brand opportunities by branching out into action figures and video games. It left its core audience—young builders—in an attempt to gain market share.

"Things started looking less like LEGO and more cool," Smith-Meyer said. "We were hiring a lot of designers known for their styling skills—designers in areas like automotive design."

The management consultants who came in to help the company streamline initiated a program called Step Up, which helped LEGO employees with higher education advance within the corporate structure. Unfortunately, many of LEGO's oldest and most experienced designers did not have the management background to benefit.

"The old designers who had been essential to bringing Drone and Star Wars to market couldn't participate in the same way, and so, much of the company lifeblood was getting lost," Smith-Meyer recalled. "It was a really bizarre time to try to keep the brick alive."

During this period, the company was working with several key assumptions. Its in-house studies concluded that kids were facing time compression, and as a result, they no longer had time to play. With all of the kids' calendars, play dates, screen time, and early academics, LEGO felt that its brick system—known for requiring a lengthy time commitment—was becoming obsolete.

The company also felt the need to compete with the instant gratification of plug-and-play toys. The digital space was bringing so many bells and whistles to the play experience, LEGO assumed that its old-fashioned bricks could not compete with the excitement.

And finally, LEGO was concerned that its traditional consumer base—young boys who like to build—was jeopardizing its ability to break into trendier markets. There was pressure to bring more-aggressive play into the brand: darker colors with more violence and danger. If the smiling yellow head of the minifigure was the face of old LEGO, the LEGO face of the 1990s and early aughts was the Navy SEAL. One German mother interviewed described the expressions on the little figures as "straight from hell."

"They wanted to move away from the nerd stigma," Smith-Meyer told us. "They were fighting the idea that LEGO was for kids who didn't have friends."

The original DNA of the company—systemic creativity through the brick—was left aside for the expansion of new product lines. With none of the modularity of core LEGO products, toys like ClickIts—an attempt to reach girls with snap-and-play accessories and jewelry—felt completely out of the LEGO family. As one LEGO employee put it, "If you covered up the LEGO logo, you would have had no sense who made that stuff."

The designers were also hamstrung by the management consultancy's new reliance on focus groups and tests. Smith-Meyer told us, "In the focus tests, kids would pick Mega Blocks, made by our competitor, simply because they were bigger. It didn't mean that kids liked them any better. They actually liked the original LEGOs better, but the focus tests were a false environment. The problem was that we were using them to inform our product development."

Despite the enormous growth in product offerings, there was an increasing sense of unease throughout the company. Instead of speaking to the real LEGO fans, the expanded brand offerings were communicating with theoretical consumers.

"We had a phrase we used to call the 'crisp, cool wow,'" Smith-Meyer said. "It was a way to describe what we thought of as wasted creativity. At the beginning of a season, we would show a hundred concepts, and it was almost like this creative fairground. We would always joke about how certain concepts would get the response, 'Wow . . . Cool . . . Yeah . . . Go for it!' We would say, 'What rationale is that? What does that mean?' We were up against the 'crisp, cool wow' because we thought it was more important to ask, 'Do we really need that? Does that add to the portfolio? Do we even *like* that?'"

By expanding the brand, LEGO was also diluting marketing opportunities for nostalgia with parents. Suddenly all the LEGO toys looked different, and there was no longer the pleasurable memory trigger for parents: *I used to play with these when I was a kid!*

"I was sitting in one of our focus groups in Germany," Smith-Meyer recalled. "And they were bringing in new moms who had kids in the right age range for our consumer base. The moms who played a lot with Playmobil, well, their kids were into Playmobil. The moms who played more with LEGO, guess what? Their kids were more into LEGO. And then there were moms who grew up in East Germany. They said, 'Oh, we didn't have a lot of toys growing up so we just played with what was around. A doll. An old teddy bear.' And they, too, said, 'Oh, my kids just play with whatever is around.'"

The play culture is an emotional link between generations just as much as it is an interaction between the kids themselves. Like our examples of the Coke bottle and the hammer, objects like LEGO bricks become most interesting when they sit in relationship to the humans playing with them. Nostalgia exists in a world of aspects, not properties. For that reason, parents were not always able to articulate to marketers their desire to see versions of their own toys, but they instantly responded when the toys looked familiar.

"Of course, our researchers said, 'No, you can't talk about nostalgia. There is no evidence to back that up . . .,'" Smith-Meyer told us. "But just look at the number of parents who grew up with LEGO. When we make a fire station that looks like the fire station that parents played with as children, it sells. When it doesn't trigger that memory, the parents say, 'Do you have something that looks a little different?' There are all these layers to product development that you can't see. Especially not if you just look at it from a management perspective or just at the spreadsheets. If you don't actually understand the ecology of play."

By the end of 2004, LEGO was adrift in a fog. After 2003, a year with an enormous deficit, 2004's heavy writedowns caused CEO Knudstorp to change course. As a sensitive environmental scanner, Knudstorp could feel that something was wrong. Using default thinking, he knew that LEGO needed to cut costs by becoming more efficient with better operations. But he also intuited that something else was being lost beyond just numbers. There was the more elusive loss of *connection* with the core of the brand. This was something deeper than simply adding new product lines or renegotiating floor space with the retailers. Knudstorp announced that the company needed to understand children's desires in a much deeper way. LEGO didn't just need to redesign its toys to sell better. It needed to understand the phenomenon of play.

Phase 2: Collect the Data

For LEGO, collecting data involved different methods for different situations: participatory observation, interviews, study of objects, narratives, card sorting, diaries, video, and photo ethnography.

Knudstorp recognized that if he truly wanted to investigate a phenomenon as deep and rich as play, he would need to enlist the help of experts. He sponsored initiatives to embed trained research teams—referred to as the LEGO *anthros*—with families in the American cities and suburbs of Los Angeles, New York City, and Chicago and the German metropolitan areas of Munich and Hamburg. The teams collected data for months. LEGO made photo diaries, interviewed parents, and asked kids to sort pictures and tell stories about the images. They spent weeks going where the kids went and analyzing the semiotics of the popular movies and stories that made up the kids' world. The teams interviewed experts on learning and child development while studying toy shops, indoor play spaces, and playgrounds. They went shopping with grandparents and parents as well as with children and the kids' friends.

Smith-Meyer explained how this data-collection process began to open up new questions for the executives at LEGO:

> The process was very different for us. Usually we would just look at the trends and develop our products and then show them to the kids in focus groups. It was always centered around this idea of, "Hey, so how cool is that . . . ?" Or, "Is this cooler than that?" Then we would wait to see what the kids would say.
>
> It's very different when you visit people in their homes. In focus groups, ten moms are sitting around in a circle in some generic space, and there is inevitably some kind of competition. There is some pressure to say what they think they are supposed to say, or not say. In a home, you get much closer to the real truth. You see more of what is happening and not what they wish or hope to project. You see that the toys are everywhere and it's a mess.

In short, the analysts were steeped in the culture of the families. As ethnographers, they did everything possible to simply observe the culture without any preconceived notions. Then, once the data was collected, the team processed every bit of raw, qualitative data in a software program. This meant that all written texts, audio recordings, videos, and graphics—once unstructured—were now coded into themes. The software program allowed the analysts to create and then manipulate networks with the themes. By mapping out all of the possible relevant patterns, the teams were ready to begin exploring the complex phenomena hidden inside the textual and multimedia data. Rather than delivering the data raw, or simply listing it, the researchers made sure the data was organized in a structured, transparent way so that the teams might identify patterns from the visuals maps.

Phase 3: Look for Patterns

Once the data is collected, sorted, and made available, the next phase is to analyze it and find the patterns. The goal is to find bigger themes that connect the data, using a process called *formal indication*. This team process is built around creative and analytical conversation.

The research team members immersed themselves in the data through conversations. "We were constantly asking, 'What is that kid doing over there? Is that the same as what this kid is doing here?'" one member of the team told us. After an intense period of discussion about the data, each researcher stepped away and made his or her own decision about the most important patterns. The researchers brought a whole lifetime of critical training to the pattern recognition process, but they also brought themselves. They melded art with science by using their own perspectives to discern the experiences of the children.

When all of the researchers came back to the conversation, they shared their choices. "Once we started deciding on the patterns," one team member said, "we kept saying to one another, 'Is this really supported by the data?' Then we would go back and check to be certain."

"You need to think about it and talk about it," said one of the researchers. "We didn't say, 'Okay, first we are going to decide, and second, we are all going to vote, and third, we are going to move on to the next step.' The process was much more nonlinear."

During a session with the photo diaries, for example, the researchers noted that the children's bedrooms in New Jersey tended to be meticulously designed by the mothers. "They look like they're from the pages of *Elle Décor*," noted one participant. Another child's bedroom in Los Angeles was suspiciously tidy with a stylish airplane mobile hanging down. "That looks staged," an anthropologist observed, and the team discussed what that might mean. These were children who were driven everywhere in SUVs with carefully managed after-school activities. The researchers noted that the moms were also "staging" their children's development. They were trying to shape children who were creative, fun, outgoing, humorous, intelligent, and quiet all at the same time. Throughout the conversation, critical theory from the human sciences provided a framework for the observations. The researchers discussed how these "staged" childhoods resembled Foucault's "panopticon," where activities were under surveillance and subject to disciplinary measures. One of the analysts drew a picture with a large circle and a very tiny circle. "This is the space we used to have for playing," he said, pointing to the large circle, "and this ever-diminishing circle is the space these kids have right now."

In this same session, several researchers reported that children were hiding things from their parents. The observers noted the acronym POS (parent over shoulder) so prevalent in online gaming. One researcher reported being invited into a young boy's room to see his most secret prized possession. The child pulled a shoebox out from under the bed and announced that it was filled with magic poisonous mushrooms.

"We asked one kid to design his ideal room," another researcher told us. "And it had all sorts of covert elements: booby traps and CSI [from the *Crime Scene Investigation* TV series] secret doorways. Everything was communicating, 'Stay out!'" The anthropologists discerned that the box of mushrooms and the booby-trapped room were both reactions against the staging and surveillance happening in the children's lives. After further discussion, the team saw a pattern emerge more clearly: the children were suffocating.

"These kids were bubble-wrapped," one team member recalled. "Every physical space in their life was curated, managed, or staged by an adult. Whereas children in the past used to find freedom and an appropriate level of danger on the streets, playing on sidewalks throughout the neighborhood or roaming free in the country, these children needed to find their freedom in virtual spaces through online gaming or in imaginary zones (like the box of magic mushrooms)."

An important insight came to the group through the discussion of all of these observations. One role of play for these children was to find pockets of oxygen, away from adult supervision. The group realized that kids were desperate to sneak some element of danger into their lives. If the researchers had used a more linear process—one focused on the properties of the children's play—the team would never have thought to put poisonous mushrooms and booby traps in the same category. But the nonlinear act of connecting the dots revealed that the underlying phenomenon of both behaviors was the same.

At another point in the discussion, the researchers reported that kids in both Germany and the United States had systems of rankings and hierarchies everywhere. One researcher told the group about a boy's elaborate game of ranking his fantasy football players. The boy could rattle off endless statistics about every one of his imaginary players. Another anthropologist talked about the almost incessant discussion of video game scores within a group of boys. He reported that every day seemed to bring a new assessment of the hierarchy based on the video game's rankings. The research team turned again to the phenomenon: what did the kids' attention to rank say about the role of play? The team discovered that just as animals use play as a means of establishing social order and hierarchy, so too do children. They are playing to understand who is alpha and who is beta.

The most salient observation revolved around an old shoe. An eleven-year-old German boy showed a researcher his most prized possession. It wasn't a video game or a fancy new toy. It was his beat-up sneaker. He lovingly pointed out all the ridges and nooks along the side and the bottom. They communicated to his friends that he had mastered a specific skateboard trick. From this observation, the researchers discerned a larger pattern of mastery. Children play to achieve mastery at a skill. And if the skill is valuable to them, they will stick with it. The German boy's dedication to skateboarding—and the social currency it brought him—dismantled all of the earlier assumptions about time compression and children's need for instant gratification from their toys. In fact, the analysts discussed, it was the exact opposite. The most meaningful play for children seemed to involve degrees of difficulty and skill acquisition. The team dubbed this insight "instant traction versus paying your dues."

These and other findings led the researchers to identify the key patterns: children play to get oxygen, to understand hierarchy, to achieve mastery at a skill, and to socialize. The patterns were simplified into four categories: under the radar, hierarchy, mastery, and social play.

"I still have the notebook from that first workshop," Smith-Meyer told us. "I was thinking, 'Why don't we do this all the time? Why would we just sit and talk to focus groups?' LEGO has done a lot of research on play, but it almost becomes too academic. It didn't really live in people, certainly not in the management. We should have been out with families. These are the real people who use our products."

Phase 4: Create the Key Insights

Once you have the patterns, the next step is to define what they mean for business, or to create the key insights. In many cases it helps to have one organizing idea to give a clear direction and focus for strategy. In this phase, you create ideas to solve the problem at the core of the insight. These might include ideas for new products, new services, customer interactions, technology, and other improvements. If your insight has depth, you won't need a ton of imagination to create the right ideas. But it is important to look at these ideas from the perspective of the people who are going to buy, use, or interact with your products. This perspective can often be built around a value proposition that defines the benefit you are bringing to market and the vectors of innovation that you can use to guide development.

Instead of focusing on the false assumptions of time compression, LEGO started to reconnect with its core consumers: the kids who wanted to achieve mastery through LEGO play. These kids really did have the time and the desire to commit to LEGO.

Smith-Meyer explained: "When you just look at quantitative research, you say, 'The average kid doesn't have time.' But the reality is different. In reality, 40 percent of kids have a fair amount of time, while another 40 percent have no time. The average can't tell you anything. What we know is that LEGO does take time. We shouldn't take away the core idea of LEGO so that it fits into an average. We should say, 'LEGO takes time . . .' and the people who want to take that time will take that time. And the people who don't will go to Hasbro for action figures or some other kind of toy. We were trying to get rid of our core competency."

The insight about the children's desire for mastery had design implications for all the products. "Now we are making products that are proud of being LEGO," Smith-Meyer said. "If you look at the boxes, you know it's LEGO. You can't force someone to play with these bricks. The research allowed us to make a decision about who we wanted to reach. It was a decision that grew into a mantra: we're going to start making LEGO for people who like LEGO for what LEGO is."

This moment of clarity about LEGO's connection to its consumer base led to the new company motto: "Inspiring the Builders of Tomorrow" and more outreach with the fan communities, including the Adult Fans of LEGO (AFOL).

"We started going to the AFOL conventions and doing business with people from the community," Smith-Meyer said. "These people were much more multifocused and dynamic in thinking about the product than we were."

The under-the-radar category that the research team had come up with helped LEGO to design toys with a covert sense of danger. One idea was a fire truck for boys—sweet and very straightforward—with an under-the-radar quality. A series of recipes would be leaked to online sites showing boys how to transform the truck into weapons and other dangerous items.

The LEGO clubhouse originated from these discussions. The clubhouse—now a central aspect of the LEGO retail environment—consists of bins and bins of LEGO bricks available for free play in all the stores. Kids can work their way up from the easiest bins—larger bricks and fewer pieces—to the hardest and most time consuming model building. Younger kids watch and learn from the older builders, creating an informal mentorship network based on a hierarchy of skills.

The patterns also showed the company where to cut back. CEO Knudstorp streamlined the elements available for new LEGO kits from 12,900 to 7,000. Instead of the design free-for-all that characterized the 1990s and the early aughts, today's LEGO product development is focused on strengthening the relationship with the same core consumer.

Executive vice president Mads Nipper described LEGO's value proposition to us:

> We've developed a strong sense around what the LEGO
> Group does particularly well—we don't want to do stuff

just because there's a market for it. There are things we choose to do and things we choose not to do. The LEGO brick and variations of it remain the core part of what we do. It's part of our DNA. When we develop new bricks or play experiences based on the system we have, we make sure everything we add to that system supports systematic creativity. If a building system is exceptionally well done, it will enable everything from a model that emerges—from two-hundred-page building instructions to an idea that it's just a creative tool with a specific collection of bricks to let you do anything you want. We believe this combination is possible; the key requirement is to make the system exceptionally well thought through.

Phase 5: Build the Business Impact

One of the insights to come out of the study had enormous profit and growth potential for LEGO. The researchers kept hearing the kids talk about going up against authority: teachers, parents, and other adults. "For the first time, I really understood Nickelodeon," a researcher told us. "Every single story on that channel shows kids rebelling. There is just a lot of energy around that idea for kids."

But when the researchers brought up the possibility to the LEGO executives, they shot it down. "That's not us," the executives told the research team. The insight had depth and market potential, but it did not appeal to the company.

"Ultimately, the business impact has to be an aesthetic and even an ethical choice for the company," one researcher noted. "It's a big credit to LEGO that they turned something like this down. It shows that they actually stand for something."

"People keep asking us to speak on how we did it," Smith-Meyer told us. "How did we make such a turnaround so quickly both internally and externally? But what they need to be asking is *why* are we doing this. Instead of asking, 'Can we make more money?' we should be asking, 'Does this add to our mission of inspiring the builders of tomorrow?'"

LEGO started its journey by reframing its problem as a phenomenon: "How do we recapture market share?" turned into "What is the phenomenon of play?" After executive leadership engaged deeply in data collection, the entire team looked for patterns, or common themes, that fit into the larger analytical framework. From there, LEGO was able to create and design key insights that gave it a genuine perspective on its market.

LEGO is not the only company to use sensemaking to obtain these moments of clarity. In chapter 6, we introduce you to the executives at Coloplast, one of the world's leading medical technology companies. Unlike LEGO, Coloplast had one specific challenge to conquer: the product-design pipeline. The company had no shortage of possible innovations—often initiated by its R&D team—but it could never adequately answer the most fundamental question: why are we making the product this way? Using the sensemaking method, Coloplast ultimately arrived at a moment of clarity that helped it create meaning and value across the entire company.

SIX

Product Design

Coloplast

A SENIOR EXECUTIVE AT A major medical supply company was looking for a new direction for one of his best-selling products. He was staring at a conference table covered with R&D proposals containing net present value calculations, but it just didn't feel right. Nothing in any of the numbers could tell him how people actually experienced the product.

He set the calculations aside and, instead, initiated a different kind of exploratory process using ethnography to study how people experienced living with his product.

When the data came back in, however, his team was overwhelmed. How do you find the needle in the haystack when you have thousands of photos, gigabytes of video, and endless field notes and other artifacts? Teasing out the reality from data like this is not as clear-cut as drafting a spreadsheet.

The executive didn't panic. Instead, he allowed his team to take its time. The team members spent months looking at the data, discussing it, and analyzing it within critical contexts. Toward the end of the exploration, the team members moved closer and closer to what the future of the product could be. They saw patterns in the data and connected them, and then, all of sudden, they experienced the moment of clarity.

When they found their core insight, it seemed obvious. Of course! It was something that all of them knew, and yet none of their launches or products ever reflected that knowledge. This clarity finally gave them a perspective: "This is the problem we are choosing to solve. This is what we stand for."

"What Problem Are We Choosing to Solve?"

Coloplast, a market leader in health-care products in Europe, was started in 1954 when a nurse named Elise Sørensen watched her sister recover from an ostomy. Though the procedure was a lifesaver—often performed on patients suffering from cancer of the stomach or colon—the resulting *stoma,* or hole in her stomach for the discharge of body waste, left her ashamed and socially isolated. Without any sort of medical device to properly address the issue, Sørensen's sister dreaded leaving the house for fear that her homemade stoma bag would leak in public. Sørensen was determined to find a solution that would restore her sister's ability to be out in public without anxiety. With a bit of engineering advice from experts, she designed the world's first ostomy bag with an adhesive ring. Once the bag was able to stay attached to her sister's skin, the danger of leakage was greatly alleviated. When she saw her sister appear at the door, headed out for a social event carrying only her hat and coat—just like any other woman on her way to lunch—Sørensen knew that a business was born.

Over the last five decades, Coloplast has stayed true to its founder's mission. Boards composed of stoma nurses make up an essential part of the innovation process. And the company, now well known for providing the highest-quality products, leads the global market for chronic ostomy and continence care, what it deems "intimate healthcare products."

In the hushed hallways of the corporate headquarters in Humlebæk, Denmark, small museum displays showcase early models of stoma and incontinence bags from the midcentury. It is a private world—once infused with shame and embarrassment—now openly displayed and rightly celebrated. The twin sensibilities of pragmatism and deep respect for the consumer imbue every corner of the Coloplast offices and speak volumes to Coloplast's historic success as a premium provider in the market.

By the late aughts, however, competition in the medical technology space was encroaching on Coloplast's lead. The company had not changed much to adapt to new market dynamics, a fact that was eventually borne out in the numbers. In 2008, the company, which had been growing in the double digits, never missing a target for fifty years, missed its sales targets four times in *one year*. The entire enterprise had steered completely off course. A new CEO, Lars Rasmussen, was brought on board, and Coloplast initiated a deep investigation of its marketing and innovation processes to evaluate where and how things went so wrong.

Rasmus Moller, newly minted vice president of global marketing in ostomy care at Coloplast, was keenly aware that his department needed an overhaul. He wanted to be the one to offer the killer insight to his colleagues. But what was the value proposition, exactly? Despite throwing himself into his work and becoming familiar with every new product coming down the innovation pipeline, he found it next to impossible to answer the most fundamental question of all: "What problem are we trying to solve?"

When Moller joined the ostomy care department in 2009, he saw vestiges of the chaos that had come before. "It was a feature nightmare," he told us. "There were too many new products coming down the pipeline, and each of them tried to improve on one or two features at a time, with no sense of a greater purpose. They were all driven by engineering and technology innovation. When we asked, 'Why do you want to improve upon this? the only answer anyone could give us was, 'Because it's better . . .'"

What Moller and his colleagues were seeking was a *perspective* on the market. The department was getting overwhelmed with feedback from the stoma care nurses about what ostomy care patients needed. In trying to solve all the problems all the time, Coloplast wound up solving nothing in any meaningful way. It had lost touch with the core experience that linked ostomy care patients to Coloplast's products. What's more, the "feature nightmare" was costing the company a fortune, as there were so many new products and no clear blockbusters.

It was time to step off the path of the more traditional, linear business models. Coloplast—and the ostomy care group specifically—was ready to go on a journey, to "wallow in the data," as one Coloplast employee put it.

"Our goal was to find a perspective so we could answer the question 'Why are we doing this?'" Moller told us. "We wanted to be able to say, 'If you work with Coloplast, this is what we will solve for you.' The nurses will always have ideas about improvements: 'What about noise from the bags or skin fit or this or that? . . .' A perspective allows us to say, 'Those are important things, but those are not the things we are choosing to solve.'"

Kristian Villumsen, now senior vice president of global marketing at Coloplast, started his career at McKinsey in the firm's Copenhagen office. Although he enjoyed the problem-solving aspect of his consulting work, he was ultimately dissatisfied by the result:

> The underlying idea in most of the work we did was that problems could be defined, broken down, and then solved. The pitfall with that approach—hypothesis-driven problem solving—within a limited time frame is that, sometimes, it became a guessing game. There was not a lot of time for discussion and no real culture for making mistakes— exploring—or getting it wrong at first. The psychology of most of the people who work at McKinsey was, "We were hired to give our clients the *right* answer." These are people who have been getting the answers right since the day they started school. There was only so much room in the budget, so sometimes a study would only last three months when it might better have lasted six or nine months. We had to solve the defined problem, but we spent so little time asking the most important questions: "Is this really the right problem to be solving? What are we actually trying to understand?"

When Villumsen was offered the opportunity to move from being a partner at McKinsey to Coloplast, his former client, in 2008, it seemed like a perfect opportunity to take on the challenge of solving business problems in a different way. But he had his work cut out for him: "The CEO was fired soon after I arrived, and the company was in dire straits, fires all over. There was no clear agenda and no direction. I started to think I had screwed up my career." Villumsen said that he decided to use the atmosphere of upheaval to initiate a long-term, more in-depth qualitative study:

There was a ton of data available but very few insights and next to no perspective, considering that the company had been in the field for fifty years. We spent millions on market research, but when we got it back, we would say, "How many markets are measured here, or what product did you use?" And either it was too old or people just didn't remember. In one study, they wanted to measure what was important in stoma care so they took 250 different factors and they asked a thousand people to rank them. It was complete crap. And it turned out that leakage was the problem. Well, we already knew that leakage was the problem. I was trying to get beyond that, get to a genuine idea, an explanation about something.

Sensemaking Applied to a Specific Challenge

Like Moller, Villumsen felt that the basic reason for Coloplast's presence in the ostomy care market was unclear. It wasn't that people at Coloplast didn't know how to solve problems—decades of cutting-edge engineering and engaged research and development teams were on board to do that—but they didn't know which problems they were trying to solve. They needed to begin the sensemaking method with phase 1, as described in chapter 5: *reframe the phenomenon.* Coloplast changed its focus from "How do we sell more products?" to "What is our consumers' experience with ostomy care?"

At Villumsen's call, a team of social science researchers then began phase 2: *collect the data.* Dispatched to live with ostomy care patients all over the world, they observed stoma care patients with their friends and family, on the streets getting around, and, perhaps most importantly, in moments when they were trapped at home. In addition, the researchers gathered insights and observations from six hundred stoma care nurses. All of this raw data was delivered back to Villumsen, Moller, and other members of the Coloplast team in the form of videos, diaries, photographs, poems, and other artifacts. There was not a single PowerPoint in sight.

"The data collection phase turned out to be much more creative and much more *real*," Villumsen said. "Usually studies produce classic examples of graphs and charts, but they are almost meaningless in the end. Some of the material I got exposed to in the sensemaking method was so raw, I could pick up the photographs and the diaries, page through them, feel them. I really looked at the bodies in the photographs. This data had a completely different texture to it."

Coloplast was deep in the midst of the sensemaking method, but the insights—and their quest for a market perspective—did not come quickly or easily. Villumsen explained:

> With this kind of work, you need to allow yourself to experience what you can from the data. And if you don't get confused, you probably need to sit with it for a longer time.
>
> Navigating all those different sources of data and forming a perspective or an interpretation from them involves both judgment and analysis. It becomes an aesthetic process. It is a function of one's experience, training, and temperament, really. Do you allow yourself enough time to experience your data before forming an opinion on the material?

Coloplast—Villumsen, Moller, and their colleagues—was ready to begin. They steeped themselves in the data sets with trained researchers, immersing themselves in the lives of the stoma care patients. They attempted to reflect on the phenomena of the care without any preconceptions, not an easy task for people trained in a culture of linear problem solving.

"I am very impatient and I wanted to form an opinion fast," Villumsen told us. "I even had some conclusions before we started, and the researchers had to tell me to 'just wait! Wait and see . . .' There was a huge benefit to allowing myself to explore."

Some of the patients expressed frustration, whereas others spoke of shame or embarrassment. One spoke about the moment he first showed his stoma bag to a new romantic partner; another described the intimate relationship between her ostomy care and her husband. Many of them mentioned that horrifying moment—at a wedding, a business meeting, in class—when they realized their stoma bag was leaking.

The data immersion phase offers specific insights about specific individuals. It is subjective without being myopic, but it does not yet have the analytical robustness to scale up and apply to a larger data set. So, after a rich exploratory period with the data, it's time to look beyond the context-dependent layers and search for discernible patterns. This is phase 3: *look for patterns*. Just like in the natural sciences, data needs to be analyzed, combined, and put into patterns and perspective before it can offer any meaning.

Genevieve Bell, profiled in chapter 7, is an anthropologist and the most powerful social scientist at Intel. She insisted that it is the interpretative lens—looking for patterns and building the key insights—and not the data sets or the numbers in the cohort that lend the process its power and relevance.

"Without the theory, anyone can do field work," she told us. "Not everyone can do it well, but you can train most people to do it. What you can't train people to do is analysis. And without analysis, you simply have reportage. At that point, you're just as well off with focus groups. Why bother without the analysis. You have to have an interpretive lens."

According to Bell, "anytime you're in someone's home, all the things they're not saying are as important as what they are saying.

The hesitancies, the body language, what is put with what in the objects of their home. All the unspoken things that lead to an observation like, 'I know this person *said* that they love your product but when we open the drawer in which all their products live, your product is still in the box.' So what is it that they love? If you don't use an analytical lens to answer that question, you're just transcribing what people say, and that won't tell you a thing about the way the world works. If what people said was true, the world would be a different place."

Even here, well into the process, it is common to make mistakes and false moves. In fact, it is an integral part of the process. The Coloplast team worked with the researchers to build a model around how the different observations connected. At one point, they tried to play with the theory that ostomy patients were scared of their stomas.

"It may have been true that people were afraid of their stomas, but it didn't explain anything," Villumsen said. "It didn't take us to any real moment of clarity. The theory needed to show us something, and there was nothing explanatory in those early insights."

"It wasn't the aha! moment," Moller told us. "There are a lot of things I can care about on a rational level, but I needed to *feel* something about this insight."

The pattern recognition phase might reveal more, giving shape to some bigger pieces or themes that relate to one another. But it is not yet totally coherent.

"The nurses kept saying things in the data like, 'There is no perfect product, because there is no perfect patient,' or 'It's a good product but it's not right for everyone,'" Moller recalled. "We could see that there was something there, but we didn't have any clear path to solving the problem. 'No perfect product?' What the hell does that mean? Does that mean we are developing roughly two million different products? That is obviously not feasible, so what are we talking about, then?"

Although counterintuitive, it is often at this late stage in the process that the greatest confusion sets in. The themes and patterns are emerging, and there are bits and pieces to assemble, but there is no overarching theory or interpretation to give it clarity. It's akin to the experience of looking at an out-of-focus photograph. All the elements are present, but you still need that core insight to snap it all into view.

The Coloplast team members were experiencing this very state of uncertainty or lack of focus. And then the key insight dawned on them: *The bodies are different.* The R&D teams were focused on creating technologically advanced polymers and adhesives, but none of these innovations—containing all the feature nightmares— were addressing core concerns. The team came to realize that people with stomas really do have different bodies. They have surgery scars and bumps; some people have lost a great deal of weight, whereas others have gained a great deal. This diversity was leading to all the complaints of compliance and leakage issues. R&D was using technology-driven innovation to design for the perfect body—imagine the mannequin model in the store—while the stoma patients came in all shapes and sizes.

"People with a hernia," Moller reflected, "have a bulging stomach, and it's very hard to attach stoma bags, but [these people] only make up 20 percent of the market. We were fixated on making products for the remaining 80 percent of the market. Once we started saying that the *bodies are different,* however, we understood that there is no 80 percent. The bodies are different, so the niches are the mainstream."

Villumsen expanded on this explanation:

> The entire industry has been talking about stopping leakage.
> It didn't translate into everything we did, because we thought

we had solved it—so a lot of innovation was happening around other, more marginal benefits: sound, smell, looks, et cetera. The research was this huge wake-up call to us— we hadn't solved it. And it wasn't just us. Nobody had. It was astounding—an entire billion-dollar industry claiming to have solved the basic issue, and then when you actually looked at it closely . . . they, we, all of us just hadn't. We had to come back to something incredibly basic, and once we did, we realized that the answer was staring us in the face: *the bodies were different*. We understood that everything we did had to be about body fit. From one moment to the next: everything clicked. It was just so obvious—so true. This simple idea brought direction and structure to everything. This gave us the confidence to start over with our product pipeline. In many ways, this gave me the foundation to lead from, a way to judge and distinguish good from bad, a way to care.

The moment of clarity.

All the disparate pieces clicked into focus for the Coloplast team. The key insight was more widely applicable and more replicable than the single-point observations, and it could be validated in larger samples. Most importantly, this insight allowed Coloplast to move forward into building the business impact.

"When we were able to distill it down [to] 'Bodies are different, and the products are not,' I really felt the power of the insight," Moller recalled. "It was a perspective that allowed me to take action. I felt I could move something with it and energize other people to change."

Coloplast started to put different body types into categories. By conducting a body study—asking a thousand users to send in photos of their bodies in different positions—the company looked at ways of grouping together the different bodies. It turned a bespoke market of millions into a market for a few stoma care body types. The products are now designed to meet the specific performance challenges of a few types of bodies. Gone are the days of the latest high-tech adhesive and cutting-edge rubber: the feature nightmare. Only a few select products make it through the pipeline now, and only if they comply with one of the body-type categories.

"People feel, perhaps for the first time, that there is a clear reason why we work with ostomy care," Moller told us. "At the sales force meeting in France, after we announced the BodyFit concept and the body types, everyone stood up and started clapping. If you have a good perspective, it is very easy to be excited about it.

––––––––––

When Villumsen and his team found a key insight, what they really discovered was a meaningful distinction—their perspective—in the market. They couldn't solve every problem with their product design, so they chose to solve the one that mattered most.

In the next chapter, we will look at how companies like Intel and Adidas use the theoretical framework of the human sciences to create meaningful distinctions across the entire enterprise. For these companies, moments of clarity have led to radical cultural shifts affecting every business in the corporation. Now that Intel and Adidas regularly use open-ended inquiry to solve problems, they exemplify a paradigm shift in the business world at large. We call this the era of *perspective-driven innovation.*

SEVEN

Corporate Strategy

Intel and Adidas

IN THIS CHAPTER, we introduce two very different methods of perspective-driven innovation happening at two vastly different companies. At Intel, Genevieve Bell, the most powerful and influential social scientist in the industry, is leading a revolution from within. Through her determined efforts, Intel is making a radical shift, moving away from the engineering-focused innovation of computing toward user experiences. Bell must use every tool in her human-sciences arsenal—from ethnography to phenomenology to pattern recognition—to articulate this new perspective both inside and outside the company. And while Bell's vision is shaping the future of Intel, her journey also exemplifies the obstacles inherent to any large-scale shift in strategy.

Meanwhile, James Carnes, creative director for sports performance at Adidas, is facing an entirely different kind of challenge. By 2004, Adidas had become enormously successful at churning out ever-more products and making money for its shareholders, but it had lost the connection with its origins. If Intel is looking for a perspective on the future, Adidas discovered that it needed to look to the past. Although executives like Carnes were well aware of Adidas's founder, Adi Dassler, it wasn't until they uncovered a tangible artifact of his strategic vision that they realized how far they had drifted. With Dassler's notes as the culmination of its open-ended inquiry, Adidas managed to reenergize its relationship with consumers while, at the same time, delivering tenfold on its shareholder profits.

Intel: The Future of Computing Is Experiences

In the late 1990s, the Intel Corporation, the world's largest semiconductor chip maker, started a small research division called People and Practices Research Laboratory. The group of social scientists involved—including a handful of cultural anthropologists, cognitive psychologists, and linguists—used the theoretical tools of their training to transform an engineering and technology-driven company into an organization dedicated to focusing on the needs and wants of the actual users. By September of 2011, little more than ten years later, then-CEO of Intel, Paul Otellini, officially announced to his company that the future of computing was no longer about PCs but rather mobile phones, embedded devices, tablets, data, and the cloud. His keynote speech culminated in a giant PowerPoint slide that read "The Future of Computing Is Experiences."

You might think that the progress from small research lab to shrewd, forward-thinking adaptation on the part of such a technological heavy like Intel was a planned strategy developed after meticulous process-oriented research. And you would be wrong. The following pages present another way to look at Intel's story.

A Woman Walks into a Bar . . .

Today, Genevieve Bell is the most powerful and influential social scientist at Intel—director of the Interaction and Experience Research Group, and one of the most respected thinkers in the industry. Back then, in 1998, she was an ex-pat Australian who had just finished up her PhD in cultural anthropology at Stanford. She was out for a night of stiff drinks in Palo Alto, trying to help a heartbroken friend drown her sorrows. Bell, in her forties, has a bounty of charisma and a disarmingly candid nature that she characterizes as "typically Aussie."

"Some guy at the bar was trying to pick up my friend," she recalled, "and I got stuck talking with the bloke with him. He asked me what I did, and I told him I was an anthropologist. He said, 'What can you do with that?' and I explained: research, teaching, all that good stuff. He said, 'You seem interesting,' and I said, 'Don't take this personally, mate, but you really don't.'"

The "bloke"—who turned out to be a Silicon Valley entrepreneur on his third start-up—remained undeterred. The next day, Bell received a call at her apartment. He had tracked down her home number by calling every anthropology department in the Bay Area.

"He said, 'I want to offer you a job,'" Bell told us. "I said, 'I've already got a job,' and he said, 'I want to offer you a better job because you still seem interesting.' And then I said, 'Well, you still don't seem interesting, and now you are starting to seem increasingly weird.'"

He finally won her over with an offer of free lunch—music to a freshly minted PhD's ears—and Bell headed out for the meeting that ultimately led to a major redirection in her career. After wowing the man's colleagues, she was eventually recruited by a curious Intel research branch called the Intel Architecture Labs. It was tucked away in Portland, Oregon, far from the busy hum of Silicon Valley's technology-driven culture.

"My direct boss," Bell said, "was a woman named Chris Riley, a psychologist who had come on board from Bell Labs. Her group was called the End-User-Driven Concept Group. When she told me that name, I said, 'I don't even know what that means.' We rebranded it as People and Practices Research Lab as soon as we could."

The work being done up in Portland was an anomaly for Intel. When Bell came on board, six of the eight people in Riley's group had PhDs in the social sciences. While the Silicon Valley headquarters of Intel was famous for its 9 a.m. "march of the nerds"—long lines of men entering the building replete with pocket protectors and ballooning khaki pants—Riley's lab was notably casual. It wasn't unusual to see the social scientists sporting Birkenstocks and jeans. Even more important, it was clear from the moment that Bell came on board that Riley's group wanted to talk about how people actually experienced technology—the way they worked and played in their ordinary lives—and not the engineering. But the lab, and the larger research institute supporting it—Intel Architecture Labs—could not articulate to Bell what they were looking for.

"They didn't know why they had hired me," Bell recalled. "Craig Kinnie, one of the founders of the lab, understood that the world was changing. At that time, in 1998, PCs were moving into the home, and [the researchers] understood that they knew nothing about the home. They also sensed that their market was about to go global and they had no idea what that might mean. So they were pretty in tune with what they didn't know. Bringing social scientists on board was their way of gaining insight into some of these unknowns."

The most forward-thinking management at Intel could see that the company was headed into a fog. The status quo of the computing industry was about to be superseded by seismic shifts in people's attitudes and behavior toward the computational interface. Though Intel's technology continued to be cutting-edge, there was no clear indication that the consumer market had any interest in following its innovations.

"On my first day," Bell recalled, "my new boss said, 'We need your help with two things. The first one is women.' I said, 'Which women?' and she said, 'All women.' And I asked her, 'All three point two billion of them? What do you want to know?' She told me that they needed to know what women wanted. As if that weren't enough to work on, then she said, 'There's a second thing.' And I'm thinking, *men*? She said, 'The second thing we need to understand is ROW.' I said, 'What is ROW?' She said, 'The rest of the world.' So I replied, 'You would like me to help you understand women and everyone else except for the United States.' She said, 'That would be good.'"

Although the marching orders struck an absurd chord, they reflected all of the uncharted territory that Intel needed to navigate in the coming years. Could it design the same product models for everyone in the burgeoning global middle class, or did the company need to localize and design its products to be country-specific and even region-specific? Intel needed to understand user experiences at every level. It would have to put some of its engineering prowess aside and completely revamp the innovation process to reflect consumer needs.

Bell and her colleagues took on the challenge with aplomb. "A couple of us sat down together around that time and we decided we were going to change the company," she said. "We even took a pact. It meant that we—the People and Practices group—were going to have to move more than corporate management did. But we all agreed that if we worked hard enough, eventually management would meet us somewhere halfway."

And so, in 1998, from a small research outpost long beyond arm's reach from corporate headquarters, a handful of analysts trained in the human sciences signed on to redirect a company culture of over sixty thousand employees. They pledged to drive innovation by focusing on ethnographic data about human and corporate experience. With a rich history and knowledge of anthropology in business, Bell and her group knew that the only way to understand Intel's approach to cultivating emerging markets would be to understand Intel's relationship to itself. Before they could change the corporate culture, they had to analyze it.

Thus a method akin to sensemaking began as Bell and her colleagues reframed the phenomenon. The question "How is the culture of Intel different from the social sciences?" changed to "What do we all have in common?"

"In the social sciences and in humanities, we're trained to hold competing ideas in our minds without feeling the need to immediately resolve them," Bell said. "The engineering world, on the other hand, while exploratory, is always aimed at finding the best solution. Management is similar: any part of business that isn't about engineering solutions comes out of Keynesian and laissez-faire economics, which believes in rational human actors. 'A rational actor is going to optimize solutions.' Well, we know now that people don't always optimize and they are certainly not always rational."

By casting an anthropological and analytical eye on the culture of Intel, Bell and her colleagues were able to better understand the challenges at hand for changing the thinking of the management structure. Bell spoke to us about the surprising commonalities between anthropologists and business leadership today:

> I've been really struck by what it takes to be an executive at a company like Intel. Increasingly, much like in my own training in the social sciences, it requires holding these multiple competing realities in one's head at the same time. An executive has to be able to hold the reality of

what the company needs to be now with what it needs to be ten years from now, and these concepts are often at odds with one another. You also have to hold the realities of different markets in your head that have completely different formulations of success. In the US, you have to think about miles per gallon and environmentally sensitive processes, and in China you just have to go really fast. For Intel executives from a culture of engineering, this is really hard. They are taught to think that dissonance should be resolved in the design: "There is one answer, and we have to get it right."

Looking Back Can Hold You Back

By interpreting data collected throughout the corporate culture, Bell and her colleagues came to realize that Intel's long-cherished legends were holding the company back. They investigated some of the deeper myths and narratives that were so inextricably woven into the corporate DNA. Surprisingly enough, they discovered that the foundational story at Intel—Gordon Moore and the famous Moore's Law—was misdirecting innovation efforts.

"Moore's Law stated that semiconductors were going to get smaller," Bell explained, "but it didn't tell us anything about what people were going to do with them or why a consumer should be interested. It started to become increasingly clear to all of us that consumers just didn't care about the same things that we cared about. They weren't necessarily engaged in our narrative." Bell found herself asking how Intel could begin writing a narrative that focused less on semiconductors and more on identifying what consumers cared about. A large part of the challenge was about helping Intel tell a new story not only to the outside world but also to itself, a process Bell likens to "narrative talk therapy for corporations."

"How do you shape a new foundational story that moves innovation forward while preserving what is important from the past?" she asked. "Subtly changing the creation myth of a company can move the conversation forward in interesting ways. It's a different way to look at how companies get stuck."

While some of Bell and her lab's investigation delved into questions of narrative and leadership, a good portion of their open-ended inquiry entailed analyzing the nitty-gritty of the everyday rituals and routines. Just as an anthropologist in the field might study cycles of the harvest in a rural farming community or chart full-moon celebrations in a fishing village, Bell and her colleagues gathered data from the logistics of Intel's budgetary calendars and strategy launches. They became well versed in the levers of power at Intel: the decision makers, the influencers, the meetings that really mattered, and the rules that could and could not be broken. This led to perhaps their greatest insight: "If you really want to bridge the distance between business and social science, you have to be willing to move," Bell said. "Not sell out or dumb it down, but communicate your message in ways that management can process. And you have to be willing to communicate it ten thousand times: over and over and over and over again."

One of the greatest cultural divides between the initial team at People and Practices Research Lab and the engineering-driven culture at Intel involved the debate between properties and aspects, between empirical attributes and specific ways in which those attributes were documented and experienced.

At first, Intel's executives didn't know what to make of Bell and her colleagues' work. "The first couple years, we spent all our time teaching them how to evaluate us," Bell said. "In that first year, every talk we gave would start out with our introduction: 'Here is what anthropology is; here is what ethnography is; here is why you should care.' Inevitably someone would ask, 'How big is your data set?' And we would say, 'That is the wrong question.' If you are focused on 'What is my N, and is my N bigger than a thousand?' then you are not listening. Those kinds of numbers are not a helpful way of thinking about what we do." Bell's claims were not quantifiable; they were about how to take a different perspective on innovation through the humanities. Because of that, she struggled to establish a way for an engineering-oriented culture to appreciate the richness of her wildly different kinds of data.

By 2004, however, through the accretion of all of its sustained efforts, the big tanker ship of Intel started to show signs of shifting course. Bell was presenting at one of Intel's most elite planning sessions. She stood up to speak, exhorting the most senior management of the company to use consumer experience to drive innovation.

"I start talking, and no one says anything. I've got thirty minutes of material in a forty-five-minute slot because there are supposed to be questions, and I am fifteen minutes into this material, and no one is saying anything. I'm flipping through the slides—no eye contact, no nothing—and I'm thinking, 'This is going very badly . . .' And then, suddenly, Paul Otellini, who was the CEO-in-waiting at the time, puts up his hand to stop me. My breath just stops. 'Genevieve,' he says, 'Can you go back and explain that slide?' And I said, 'Yes!' Then the room just changed. Everyone sat up. They're thinking, 'All right, the next CEO is paying attention to this. We should pay attention, too.'"

Instead of cruising through the rest of the presentation, Bell actually had to go back to the second slide to address the onslaught of questions. She ended with her vision of the future: "If Intel is going to be this platform company, we're going to need to be experience-driven and we're going to have to work out how to do this *now*."

At the first break, Bell could hardly stand up. She was surrounded by members of senior management eager to follow up the discussion.

"The first one out of the gate is the guy who runs consumer electronics, and he says, 'You serious about that?' and I said, 'Of course,' and he said, 'Good! I need you. I want to do that. When can you start?' And then the next one says, 'I outrank him and I want to do that, too. I need you to come and do it for me.' And the third one says, 'You're going to go with these guys? Come with me and help my department instead!'"

Bell went to her boss and told her that the company was ready for "a change." It was time for the foot soldiers of the human sciences to fully infiltrate the company. Bell left People and Practices Research Lab, starting up her own group of twenty researchers with one of the department heads. The other members of the lab followed her, moving from the Portland office down to the main business departments in Santa Clara.

Six months later, Craig Barrett was set to attend his last meeting as the CEO of Intel. He asked Bell to give the same talk she had presented at the strategy meeting. But it was an even smaller group: three hundred of the most important decision makers and managers in the company.

"Craig gets up before I speak," Bell recalled, "and he tells the room, 'I want you to listen to this woman. She may have a funny accent and she may not be like the rest of us, but she is the future of the company, so pay attention.'"

Adidas: Athletes and Consumers Are Not Contradictory Labels

At the beginning of the book, we introduced you to a senior executive navigating in a fog. In the midst of a routine strategy session, he found himself wondering, "Is yoga a sport?" This led him to start asking the most fundamental questions about the products he was making and selling. What do we do here? How do we define ourselves? What business are we in?

That senior executive is Adidas's James Carnes, and he works out of the company's main headquarters in Herzogenaurach, Germany. Every time he crosses the campus, he sees photographs of athletes winning gold medals, cases of track shoes replete with dust from Olympic soil, and a display of the original Samba from 1950, the first shoe emblazoned with the iconic three white stripes.

His company is so steeped in history, in fact, that even members of its most senior management did not fully realize that they were in the midst of a fog until it was almost too late. Only when Adidas delved deep into a method of sensemaking did the company fully realize that its perspective on the market would bring it right back to where it started.

A Fabled Beginning Is Not Always Enough

The story of Adi Dassler, founder of Adidas, has a mythic quality about it. Dassler, a trained cobbler, wanted to find a way to make shoes for the sports heroes he so revered. An athlete himself, he was able to put himself in the mind-sets of the sports stars, imagining their specific needs on the court, the field, and the track. In 1936, Dassler sought out world-class runner Jesse Owens and designed a pair of shoes with handmade spikes for his Olympic performance at the Berlin games. Owens went on to win four medals wearing Dassler's shoes. From there, the now-famous relationship between Dassler's shoes and the elite athletic community was formed. Stars as varied as Muhammad Ali, Franz Beckenbauer, and Zinedine Zidane all sported the iconic three stripes on their way to athletic history.

But in the late 1990s, the company was starting to drift. Several mergers with other sport equipment companies meant that Adidas was under pressure to create shareholder value. Dassler's fastidi-ous attention to craft—including an on-site workshop of leather and pattern makers—was eroded when the majority of the company's manufacturing was moved off-site to Asia. Adidas's long-standing association with elite athletes was superseded by the young upstarts at Nike. These savvy newcomers were able to score endorsement contracts with superstars in basketball like Michael Jordan.

Carnes could feel the ship moving off-course, a sensation that started with subtle shifts in mood at the company. "We were still mak-ing good money," he told us. "In the United States, we were always one of the top five sports brands, but we knew something was missing. Is it distribution? Do we just need more product out there? Or do we need to talk about one story each season? The questioning process kept leading us back to the consumers: what do they need from us?"

At the time, in 2003, Adidas's approach to innovation was focused on technical advancements and improvements of shoes and apparel. Product development took place in what could be called a closed circuit between Adidas product development teams and profes-sional athletes. The assumption was decades old: the company develops products for the best athletes out there—the 5 percent—and 95 percent of sales will happen when ordinary people see the shoes on their idols, be it in soccer, basketball, or tennis.

Of course, like any other corporation, Adidas had lots of data on consumers. It knew how many hours of sports a fourteen-year-old boy would engage in every week; what colors he liked; the names of all his sports idols; how much he (and his parents) would spend on sports gear annually; and how big a share of wallet Adidas could realistically aim at getting access to vis-à-vis the other competitor brands. There was no lack of information—properties, not aspects—about its target consumer. So much so, it had a name for him: "the kid." *What does the kid want this season?*

But something was nagging at James Carnes. When he walked around on the city streets, he could see people running, going to the gym, mountain biking, carrying yoga mats. While these people seemed invested in an active lifestyle, they were not particularly fond of a specific sport. They were not organized in leagues, and they did not seem to have any classic sports idols. Instead of taking trips to the great outdoors for exercise, these people wove their workouts right into the urban fabric. So much so that every time Carnes went out on the street, he would bump into them.

What *Are* Sports?

In an attempt to gain a deeper understanding of what was going on, Carnes assembled a number of his own designers and teamed them up with human-science analysts. It was late July, and in the quiet of the summer months, Carnes could spare some of his team's time to engage in an open-ended method like sensemaking. This was not a high-level project that had been planned for months. It was not included in the annual "cycle of development projects," and it was not cleared with top management. It was simply an attempt to get a better understanding of what was going on with these urban sports-like activities. In dialogue with the analysts, Carnes reframed the phenomenon: "How do we sell sports equipment" became "What *are* sports?"

The team went out and spent in-depth time with a select group of this new tribe. After collecting data and analyzing it, the team identified a growing group of people who were highly engaged in sports without self-identifying as athletes. These people did not train to win a particular game or tournament; they trained to be fit for life. In 2003, Adidas had almost nothing to offer this particular type of consumer despite this segment's potential to form the largest consumer group for athletic equipment in the coming decade.

The sensemaking method revealed a number of patterns. Some of these echoed deeply rooted beliefs already in place at Adidas, while others challenged the entire ethos of the company. Adidas was built on offering high-performance products to athletes. The investigation revealed that urban athletes also had great expectations from their workout clothing and gear. They were willing to pay for high-performance shoes, apparel, and other gear that enabled them to perform at their best while working out. So far, so good.

But another pattern revealed that urban athletes were seeking style in their clothing. At that time, Adidas designed gear that worked extremely well at the running track or football field, but the products didn't make the consumers look particularly attractive or stylish. The company was actually promoting a fashion line of clothes and shoes, but they were designed with the nightclub in mind, not the yoga class. Most urban athletes were working out in the midst of pedestrians and shoppers, and they wanted to look good while on the "urban stage." Multicolored spandex just wasn't going to cut it for this crowd. Although Adidas had nothing in its product line that addressed these needs, a collaboration on urban sports gear with the British superstar designer Stella McCartney later changed this.

Finally, it was clear that these people contextualized their workout routine within a larger narrative. Working out, be it running, mountain biking, going to the gym, or doing yoga, was something people did as part of an attempt to live a healthier life. These same urban athletes were also deeply invested in eating food they deemed healthy, in calculating their daily intake of caffeine and other substances, in measuring their heart rate during various activities. They were looking for ways to incentivize their fitness goals: "I can eat one chocolate truffle a night if I do my whole workout," or "I will know I am successful when I can wear that little black dress

I just bought on sale." Back in 2003, sports companies were simply not part of this conversation with consumers. No sports company helped people stay motivated with structured incentives; no sports company helped consumers maintain and develop their training routines; and no sports company had a point of view on nutrition. In the urban athlete's mind, these topics, along with fitness routines, were all part of the healthy narrative, but at that time, no sports company was perceived as a credible conversation partner in the dialogue.

Carnes and his team tried to move beyond pattern recognition to key insights. Adidas needed to have a holistic approach to urban athletes, simultaneously offering them high-performance products with style while helping them stay motivated. Only by engaging in the conversation around healthful living would Adidas matter to these people. What would help Carnes's team connect all of these dots to form a moment of clarity?

The data that arrived to answer that question didn't appear on a spreadsheet or from inside a PowerPoint deck. In fact, it was hand-written on old-fashioned paper decades ago. Carnes walked into his office one day, and there it was: a photocopied collection of Adi Dassler's original notes for the company, faithfully transcribed by his assistant and now available to company employees outside the Dassler family:

> Lead, don't copy
> Quality and Creativity go hand in hand
> Always attempt to simplify every process as far as possible
> Functionality, fit, weight, aesthetics and quality make an
>   Adidas product
> Our products must always be recognizable as Adidas
>   products

"Something really hit me deep inside about the essence of the company," Carnes told us. "Dassler wasn't afraid to play on the big stage and be an impresario and be provocative, but his real personality was behind the scenes. His behind-the-scene ethic was, 'I can't be on the big stage unless I can really stand behind what I am offering these athletes.'"

Although it was years after the initial sensemaking method, finding Adi Dassler's notebook provided Carnes's team with the key insight for how to approach urban athletes. Carnes had a moment of clarity: athletes and consumers are not contradictory labels. Dassler's standards—essentially the company philosophy—gave Carnes's design team a direction and a bar against which to measure their product ideas. If urban sports are on par with basketball or soccer, Adidas must then deliver on products with functionality, aesthetics, and quality. Adidas must lead, not copy in this whole new category of lifestyle sport. Most important, every product should be recognizable as Adidas.

The foundations of the sensemaking method can vary widely from company to company. For example, while Bell and her team found that the origin story of Intel was holding them back, the narrative behind Adidas and its founder allowed Carnes and his senior management to finally connect all the dots. Adidas was created to make the best products possible for athletes, regardless of their level of professionalism.

These sensemaking insights formed the initial building blocks for a larger transition at Adidas. The company went from being a sports brand exclusively for athletes (and, coming in as a secondary target group, the rest of us mortals) to becoming an inclusive brand inviting all of us to join a movement of living a healthier and better life. It went from creating corporate credos aimed at high-performance sports aficionados, such as "Impossible is nothing," to sending democratic, yet aspirational, messages like "All In." From focusing solely on classic sports, the company now includes more broadly defined urban sports-like activities while still paying the same amount of attention to detail and performance in the product line.

Today, Carnes keeps a PowerPoint slide of Dassler's original document at the ready every time he needs an infusion of inspiration. He projects it onto the wall of his office so he can read the tiny but precise scrawl of Adi Dassler's final standard: *Only the best for the athlete.*

Intel and Adidas are arriving at new companywide perspectives by engaging in the deep, rich, and often messy work of sensemaking. This journey requires that managers learn to communicate to their colleagues. In addition to doing her work, Bell has become an expert at *explaining* her work to colleagues. The two companies demand a reliance on radically different kinds of data: Carnes and his management team were open to inspiration from Dassler's notes, and the founder's standards became a valuable piece of their sensemaking puzzle. Finally, both Bell and Carnes were attuned to marginal activity in their industries. They kept questioning, observing, and wondering, What is really happening? They communicated this spirit to their colleagues by admitting that they did not have all the answers. In their journeys, Bell and Carnes forged ahead without a hypothesis in an effort to truly experience the worlds of their consumers.

"The best anthropologists admit they don't know anything," Bell concluded. "Whenever we were approached by department heads in management, we told them we were up for anything. They would come to us with a project, and we would say, 'We have no idea how to help you, but we're going to try.' We were always game to participate because that's how the conversations start changing. 'You have a business challenge? We have no idea what the answer is, but excellent! Let's get going!'"

The road ahead for both Intel and Adidas is by no means guaranteed. If either company hopes to maintain market share by delivering on its radical shifts, it will need to constantly assess its leadership. In the following chapter, we'll discuss the unique characteristics of a leader who can engage with a problem-solving method like sensemaking. A leader inspired by the human sciences is characterized by a potent alchemy between political savvy, technological expertise, and years of experience. Although there is no easy recipe for cultivating such skills, there are certain salient attributes in all great leaders. It's not about being the most brilliant person in the room; nor is it about running all the numbers and coming up with the "right" plan. It's certainly not about living life locked up in the boardroom or the corner office, detached from the world of experiences and the behavior of your consumers.

EIGHT

How to Lead to Your Moment of Clarity

IF YOU HAPPEN TO WALK by Moses Hall on the University of California, Berkeley, campus, you will likely see a hunter-green convertible Karmann Ghia parked outside. Chances are, the top will be down. It is not unusual to see its owner riding it up and down the main drag of Berkeley, even in the rain. This car belongs to a man who is arguably the world's leading expert on phenomenology: Hubert Dreyfus.

The decor in his office is laughably simple: books on top of books on top of books. As Dreyfus is the preeminent expert on Heidegger, it's no surprise that his numerous copies of *Being and Time* are held together with thick rubber bands. An entire shelf is given over to Kierkegaard. And he admits his begrudging admiration for the works of Husserl. Outside the windows, bells chime the hour. It is the iconic academic nook, a perfect corner for giving oneself over to a life of the mind. So why are *we* here? Despite everything we have argued for throughout this book, does a master of the human sciences like Dreyfus really have anything to tell us about how to run a business? We think so. Dreyfus has spent his career promoting the idea that the ability to prioritize experiences and respond to what is most relevant is what differentiates humans from machines. This same skill—the ability to take a perspective on a problem—is at the heart of all great business leadership.

Hubert Dreyfus, now eighty-three, looks smaller and more frail than he did just a few years ago. It seems hard to believe that this was the philosopher who took on the entire computer science department at MIT in 1965. Dreyfus claimed that symbolic representational artificial intelligence would never succeed because the algorithmic design—so skilled at following rule sets—had no ability to infer or intuit. To use anthropologist Clifford Geertz's phrase, artificial intelligence was forever in the realm of thin description, completely incapable of understanding the "thick description" of our humanity. Today, such a claim seems commonplace, but at the time, Dreyfus was considered a maverick. He had never programmed a computer in his life, but his training in phenomenology and his deep knowledge of philosophy convinced him that our greatest asset as humans had nothing to do with our ability to follow rules. Humans are human because they have a perspective: they care about things. One might call it our ability to give a damn. And it is this quality that allows us to determine what matters and where we stand. A computer can't do that.

"What is relevant right now is that I am sitting here talking to you in this room," Dreyfus told us. "What is not relevant is that the room may have ten billion specks of dust on the floor and two screws in the left corner and tiles that weigh a half pound each."

The ability to have a perspective—to respond to what matters and what is meaningful—is at the heart of humanity and, by extension, at the heart of all successful businesses. A perspective implies that you have prioritized certain things—relevant things—and by consequence let some things go. This risk—letting profitable opportunities go for the sake of others—is the essence of all value propositions. We can't solve all the problems for all the consumers all the time. Nor can we design products that meet all the needs of all the people everywhere. What we can do is risk responding to what calls us. We can find ourselves committed to a perspective. We can build a successful business that will sustain us.

Dreyfus summed it up by saying, "What distinguishes the risks I'm interested in from mere bravado is that they are taken in the interest of what one is committed to, what they have defined themselves in terms of, and what makes meaningful differences in their lives. This is the kind of risk that is a necessary step in becoming a master at anything."

The sidebar "Case Study: The Television Is a Piece of Furniture" provides ample illustration of the value of committing to a perspective.

CASE STUDY

The Television Is a Piece of Furniture

It was the mid-2000s, and the executives within Samsung's TV division were in a fog. Despite all the latest technology on offer, their TVs were languishing in the marketplace. At the time, a typical Samsung TV looked much like all the others on the shelf, including those of its main competitor, Sony. All the boxes were covered with stickers touting new features, and the display models all showcased that same penetrating blue light throughout the stores. One consumer described the whole look and feel of the television buying experience as "very Star Wars." Samsung, like most other TV producers at the time, was telegraphing a message to its consumers: TVs are a piece of electronics.

And that was precisely the problem.

Although they could not yet articulate their increasing sense of unease about this assumption, the members of senior management knew that things were changing. They could feel a shift in mood from the consumers, a growing sense of dissatisfaction with the ongoing parade of engineering breakthroughs. The company could slap on ten more stickers shouting out ten more features on its latest TV, but its consumers no longer seemed able to keep up. Perhaps it was because they no longer cared.

The executives set out to investigate the problem by reframing it. They shifted the question from "How do we sell more TVs?" to "What is the phenomenon of the TV in the home?" With the guidance of a team of analysts using the human sciences, they started collecting observations: people were hiding TVs in the corner of their living rooms; women were involved in the purchase of the TV and were dissatisfied with the aesthetic experience; consumers reported that they wanted objects in their home—including TVs—with a timeless feel.

Like an image coming into focus, the insight dawned on the team members. And then, they experienced the moment of clarity. Though the TV needed to function as a form of technology, it played an additional role in the home: the TV was a piece of furniture.

Both obvious and groundbreaking, this understanding immediately gave the executive team a depth of understanding. It set about redesigning its entire product line based on its new point of view. The customers didn't want to bring home *Star Wars*. They wanted the timelessness of great furniture design. At the same time, they also wanted their TVs to have—not *all* the latest technology—but the best technology.

From there, the steps were comparatively simple. If you want to know about great furniture design, you go to Scandinavia and learn from the masters. And that is exactly what the team did. Members of the top brass at Samsung enrolled in a Scandinavian design crash course. They worked with the guidance of designers from Stockholm, Copenhagen, and Helsinki to reenvision the penetrating blue light emanating from the screen. Instead, they decided, the TV screen should give off a light evocative of a Scandinavian candle: a sense of warmth and soft, indirect light, even a hint of light through wax. The new models would have a base that hid the speakers and other eyesores like wires and buttons. They threw out the design vocabulary of big, boxy shapes and brought in iridescent white curves reminiscent of the organic shapes found in nature.

At the same time, senior management spent an enormous amount of time and resources on developing the technology within these newest TVs. With the help of cutting-edge R&D, it made big bets on reducing the size of its TVs—designing the now familiar flat screen using LEDs. This marriage between engineering prowess and newly acquired customer insights created an entirely new standard for TV design. The new Samsung models didn't just look beautiful; they also delivered on the technology benefits that mattered most to the TV-watching experience. It was the ideal marriage of form and function.

Once the senior management at Samsung had a perspective, the business implications developed organically. The company's commitment to the new perspective meant that it had to pass on various growth opportunities, and yet this never resulted in a loss for the shareholders. In fact, in 2007, following their sensemaking journey, Samsung managed to gain 11.3 percent of the TV market. By 2012, only five years later, their market share was more than double at 28.5 percent.

Today, by setting a precedent with its consumers, Samsung is the Arne Jacobsen of television design. As one consumer put it, "Samsung just feels different than Sony." As we have argued throughout this book, feelings—the experience of watching television—matters. In the midst of a fog, experience matters the most.

Samsung's success with its redesigned televisions is a shining example of the power of a method like sensemaking. By following the five phases—from reframing the problem as a phenomenon all the way through to building new business impacts—the company found a perspective on its market and has completely changed the television experience for its consumers.

Where Do We Go from Here?

At this point, you may have come to the conclusion that hiring a couple of anthropologists, philosophers, or sociologists will give your team better insights and a better sense of people and their behaviors. We sometimes refer to this approach as *drive-by anthropology* because, though hiring people with a human-science background—anthropology, history, psychology, and beyond—is often useful, it's not a silver bullet. In most of the companies we know, people with *any* background will quickly conform to the company's culture and routines. A human-science background is not some kind of magical key to unlocking the human reality or getting a better sense of customers and users. Without proper leadership—people at the helm who have chosen a meaningful perspective on the business—you probably won't change much by simply hiring a team of anthropologists. Think of Genevieve Bell at Intel: most human scientists need to be trained in business thinking and fluent in the corporate culture to make any valuable contribution.

Getting impact out of the research requires the ability to translate human-science insights into the business context and the particular business problem at hand. It requires the ability to *lead* the process. Implementing a method like sensemaking can take you part of the way, but it doesn't take you all the way.

––––––––––––

Starting any open-ended inquiry is a big endeavor. It forces you to ask some very basic questions about what business you are in as it challenges you to rediscover your relationship to your customers and users. Our own method of sensemaking is not easy. As you have already seen, it can be fundamentally counterintuitive, and it will question assumptions about your business. For that reason, the sensemaking approach will be met by a lot of resistance. But if you can get over these hurdles, it has the potential to open new worlds to your company. It can reinject a renewed sense of purpose and inspire your employees, your stakeholders, and your customers in surprising and big ways.

Considering all this, the first question to ask is, "Are we really in a fog?" Most executives can probably recognize signs of danger at some level. But in many cases, these signs are not dominating the culture of the company; these small changes in the barometric pressure will shift back of their own accord. In other cases, however, a fog is thick and dense. Is a mood of anxiety dominating the culture? As discussed throughout the book, this unease is not something you can quantify or objectively diagnose. It's a change of atmosphere that you can feel. It typically sets in with a gnawing sensation that something is wrong: you can feel it creep in and take hold when you attend presentations, meetings, and strategy sessions. *I am not comfortable with how our company understands the world around us.* This growing feeling is something you need to pay attention to; this is your intuition talking. If you feel a fog set in deep and thick, chances are it is so pervasive throughout the company and next to impossible to deal with on a case by case basis. A more fundamental approach is needed.

Two Leadership Roles: Decision Makers and Sensemakers

Leaders are often portrayed as decision makers: they sit on top of the hierarchy and make choices about the company's strategy in light of recommendations provided by the staff. When all of the facts are in, the decision maker weighs his or her options and then announces a decision. A decision makers' job is to steer the company through good times and rough times. They set the direction and vision for the entire company: they define the values and principles, set the strategic goals and priorities, and surround themselves with a team that is accountable for executing vision and strategy. But each of these tasks is fundamentally seen as a kind of decision. You decide what the vision of the company should be and what strategic priorities need to be taken. Leadership as decision making is almost seen as a kind of science or technique in itself. There is one right way to lead more effectively.

The role of the leader as a decision maker is perfectly in line with the default problem-solving model in business: hypothesis driven, quantitative, and linear. The decision maker role works well when there is a well-established relationship between cause and effect and between problem and solution. It is a highly efficient way to utilize leadership capability. The executive can distance himself or herself from the everyday operation of the business, make a vast set of decisions quickly, and trust that if the business does x, it can expect y.

Sensemaking requires a different type of leadership skill. Whereas a decision maker analyzes, a sensemaker creates. The sensemaker's job is to find new ways to compete for the business; it is about looking ahead and seeing what's next, defining new spaces to compete in, giving new meaning to the offerings of the company, and putting words to something that may not be entirely understood yet. Table 8-1 summarizes the differences between decision makers and sensemakers.

Sensemakers still need to be clear on goals and priorities. But on top of that, a new set of skills is required: the ability to lead open-ended discovery, to sense both soft and hard data, to use your judgment skills, to connect the dots, and to see the big picture in a vast ocean of sometimes conflicting data. The role of a sensemaker is, in many ways, akin to political leadership at its best. From time to time, politicians have to step out of the everyday reality of politics and look at the bigger picture. They have to remove themselves from the tactics of the political game; cut through the fog of opinions, voices, data, power battles, analysis, and advice; and create a vision

TABLE 8-1

Differences between decision makers and sensemakers

Aspect of leadership	Leaders as decision makers	Leaders as sensemakers
Primary role	Make timely and informed decisions	Discover future direction
Nature of effort	Evidence-based	Judgment-based
Primary skills needed	Analytical skills	Synthesis skills
Relationship to phenomena	Detached from phenomena	Absorbed in the phenomena
Role of data	Data gives clear answer	Data can be conflicting

for how to solve a political problem or, in some cases, the future of an entire nation. At various times in history, political leaders have shown extraordinary moments of clarity. Think of Otto Von Bismarck, who united Germany into one empire; George Washington leading the American Revolution and the founding of the United States; Franklin D. Roosevelt guiding America through the Great Depression; Gandhi taking India into freedom; Mikhail Gorbachev pulling Russia out of the cold war and into democracy. All of these leaders were able to find clarity and direction in the midst of turbulence, uncertainty, and sometimes even chaos. What can these extreme cases of leadership teach us about taking a business out of a fog?

The historian Isaiah Berlin has developed one of the most inspiring insights on leadership that we have ever come across. He spent a good deal of his life studying politics, always curious to find out what characterized great political leadership. When he was writing his books and essays—throughout the mid- to late twentieth century— many political scientists and economists were convinced that great politics was, in the end, a rational game. They believed that you could find universal laws and frameworks that might guide politicians to make the right political decisions and that such laws could encourage the entire political system to become more rational and science based. Sound familiar?

After a life spent looking at how politics actually happened, Berlin rejected the idea that political judgment could be reduced to rules or universal frameworks. Instead he found that great political leaders had a set of personal skills that he called "perfectly ordinary, empirical, and quasi-aesthetic." He argued that great political leaders had a gift of judging a particular situation according to a deep sense of reality founded by experience, an empathic understanding of others, and a sensitivity to the situation. This skill involves the extraordinary ability to synthesize "a vast amalgam of constantly changing multicolored, evanescent, perpetually overlapping data, too many, too swift, too intermingled to be caught and pinned down and labeled like so many individual butterflies."

If we follow Berlin's argument, the gift of a sensemaking leader is the ability to see patterns in a vast ocean of data, impressions, facts, experiences, opinions, and observations and to then connect these patterns into a single unifying moment of clarity. In Berlin's mind, this requires a "direct, almost sensuous contact with the relevant data," an "acute sense of what fits with what, what springs from what, what leads to what."

This ability is not an academic or analytical skill. It is a sophisticated kind of instinct that might be called "wisdom, imaginative understanding, insight or perceptiveness." It requires that you use your experience and wisdom to connect the dots between soft and hard data, between scientific facts and practical reality, between opinion and fact, between an existing situation and future possibilities.

Berlin's argument has huge consequences for what it means to lead. As a sensemaker, you cannot take yourself out of the equation. You have to absorb yourself into the problem, getting to a level where you can nearly *feel* the data confronting you. You have to see yourself as an interpreter rather than as a decider. This means you are the guide on a journey that has no clear destination: you have to accept that you don't always have *the* answer.

Leading by way of sensemaking requires the abilities that Berlin so perceptively articulated. It requires that you, as a leader, know how to ask the right questions, how to see the patterns in the data, how to make the right interpretation, and how to shape those interpretations into actions. Hiring human-science researchers or experimenting with open-ended qualitative studies will not create much impact without your direction and interpretation into the particulars of your company. And insights will be of little value if you can't put them into action.

The Three Skills of a Sensemaking Leader

Unlike the frameworks in most management theory, the leadership skills you need at the helm of a method like sensemaking cannot be learned in a business school, an executive program, or business books. It is not a technical skill; it is a practical skill that you learn through experience. Just as you can't learn to be a good football player without playing, a good carpenter without carpentering, or a good writer without writing, the good leader is forced to use experience, judgment, and wisdom.

Having said that, we have observed three fundamental characteristics of great sensemaking leadership:

1. Sensemakers care deeply about the products and services they make and the meaning that these offerings create for people.

2. Sensemakers have a strong perspective on their business—a perspective that stretches beyond the current time horizon and the current company boundaries.

3. Sensemakers are good at connecting different worlds inside the company. An organization should have a diverse set of skills to understand the big idea, translate it into action, and maintain the operation.

Leading with Care

Not long ago, we met an executive from a global pharmaceutical company. He had been participating all day in a workshop on the future of health care and was standing outside the hotel, catching some fresh air. We talked about how the health-care business was changing and what challenges the company was facing with rising health-care costs, low R&D productivity, and a broken sales model. We asked him his thoughts on the challenges ahead.

He looked at us with somewhat tired eyes, squinted up in the sky, and said, "Well, first, I am going to have myself a big, fat sushi dinner, and then I suppose I will get back to the office tomorrow and do the usual stuff—you know: hire some people, fire some people, and make some strategies."

He was not being ironic. He was being brutally honest about a feeling that many executives feel from time to time: *What does it matter, anyway?* Over time, as management has become increasingly professionalized, you can sense a kind of nihilism or loss of meaning in the executive layers. This sense of nihilism is strongest in large corporate cultures where management is seen as a profession in and of itself with no strong connection to what the company actually makes or does. What happens when satisfaction from work comes from managing—reorganizing, optimizing the operation, hiring new people, and making strategies—and not from producing something meaningful? How do you feel when it doesn't really matter whether you make beauty products, soft drinks, fast food, or musical instruments?

If you feel vulnerable to this kind of despondency, you are not well positioned to lead your company out of a fog. Remember that a method like sensemaking is neither linear nor mechanical. There is no machine to number-crunch the data. Actually, there isn't even one right result. You, as a leader, have to make sense of the insights and connect them to the problem at hand. That requires an ability to create the meaningful distinctions Hubert Dreyfus described. When you choose a perspective, you intuitively sense what's important and what's trivial, you can see what connects with what, and you have the data, input, and knowledge that matter. Caring is the connective tissue that makes all these things possible.

If you are in the beauty business, you simply can't make sense of deep insights on beauty ideals if you don't care about the meaning of beauty products. If you are in the car industry, you have to care about cars and transportation—otherwise, the human phenomenon of driving does not make sense at all. Without care, you will see everything as properties, or what Isaiah Berlin called "so many individual butterflies."

For philosophers like Dreyfus, all this is old hat. Martin Heidegger, for example, claimed that care—or what he called *sorge*—is the very thing that makes us human. He didn't mean care as an explicit emotional connection with things or people. He meant care in the sense that something matters to you, that something is deeply meaningful to you. It is this care that enables us to interact with stuff in the world in very complex ways and to see new ways of interacting with the world.

Care is such a fundamental human condition that it is noticeable in an instant—as is its absence! When you walk into an IKEA store, you know instantly that someone cares about making contemporary design furniture available for people at low prices. You see evidence of care in both senses of the word, in terms of *mattering* and *carefulness*: in the meticulous organization of the store, it is evident that the creators of the store were deeply invested in its mission. You can see it in the way the store has been designed—it is not the nicest store in the world, but it does its job incredibly well. You are led through IKEA much as you would be led through a museum of interior design. The products are shown in their context, so that a whole kitchen looks like it would look in your home; it's not just a bunch of individual cupboards, tables, and chairs. You can see it in the products; they fit nicely into most homes, and someone has taken the utmost care in design to get them down in price without sacrificing too much on the aesthetic side. You can see it in small details like the names of the products. For the most part, all items are named according to a system developed by IKEA where each type of item carries a different name origin. For example, dining tables and chairs are generally named after places in Finland, while carpets are named after places in Denmark.

The management of IKEA is known for its attention to detail; every single thing is thoughtfully considered. There is a constant focus on cost control and product development. The founder, Ingvar Kamprad, is notorious for cost-consciousness in his own life. Even though he has a net worth of $45 billion, he drives an old Volvo 240, recycles tea bags, collects salt and pepper packets at restaurants, and is regularly seen in IKEA stores having a cheap meal. He explains his philosophy in his book *Testament of a Furniture Dealer*: "It is not only for cost reasons that we avoid the luxury hotels. We don't need flashy cars, impressive titles, uniforms or other status symbols. We rely on our strength and our will!" Since its foundation in 1947, IKEA has managed to lower its prices by 2 to 3 percent annually. No wonder nearly half a billion people visit the big blue warehouse each year.

You can find care everywhere. You can find it in your local grocery store, in your city library, in kindergartens, in sushi restaurants, in computer games, and even in the way the sewage system works. In places with care, you can just sense that the people working there are deeply involved in what they do; it matters to them.

Care—both a sense of investment and carefulness—is not something you can install in your organization the way you install a new application on your mobile phone. You can't order it the same way you order a meal in a restaurant. Neither is it something you can force through by writing down your values or your vision. Care is not explicit, like a manual, a recipe, or a headline in a newspaper. When people care about something, they often can't even explain it. If you have ever heard an interview with an epic soccer player like Lionel "Leo" Messi, it is downright disappointing. You get ninety minutes of god-like ballet on the soccer field, where you see him perform tricks you thought were impossible, but his explanation is often painfully dull and linear: "I always try to do what I think is the best thing: to head towards the opposition's goal and from there it all comes naturally."

Care shows itself when it is exposed to the right conditions. If you sense that you may lack care or if your focus is entirely on the financial performance of your company, it will help to expose yourself to the qualities of what your company produces. Here are a couple of ways to develop care:

- Become a consumer of your own products, and try to put yourself in your customers' shoes. Go where they go, and sense what it is like to be serviced by your organization.

- Spend a couple of days on the floor of the company, and try to work in different positions. If you are in the car rental industry, for example, try to work as a service officer for a few days. Try to be the guy or gal who cleans the cars; try to work in your hotline or even in the IT department.

- Meet people across the organization, and talk to them about what they do when they enjoy work. Observe what matters to people in your company.

- Read the magazines, blogs, and books that your customers and colleagues read. Attend the events they would attend, and try to sense what is driving their behavior.

- Ask people in your organization which colleagues are very special to the company. It might be a computer scientist who writes code like poetry. It might be an engineer who has spent nine years developing a new feature. It might be a service manager who gets fan letters from the customers. Engage yourself in their world.

After exposing yourself to the qualities of what your organization produces, care will probably reveal itself to you the same way you learn a language. First you will learn the basic structure of the language, then you will be able to construct small sentences, and, after a while, you will just speak it without thinking. When you reach this level of fluency, you don't have to think about what matters. Cultivating care will have become a part of you.

Leading with Perspective

It can feel a little too obvious to mention Steve Jobs as a great business leader, but he *is* a good example of a leader who had perspective. In Walter Isaacson's best-selling biography, Jobs describes his perspective on technology this way: "I always thought of myself as a humanities person as a kid, but I liked electronics. Then I read something that one of my heroes, Edwin Land of Polaroid, said about the importance of people who could stand at the intersection of humanities and sciences, and I decided that's what I wanted to do."

The idea of standing at the intersection of technology and humanities is a very original concept of how technology should be designed and what it should do for its users. It is not self-explanatory, as is a statement like "We want to make computers that are easy to use." Rather, the idea of an intersection is a metaphor for an entirely new way to think about technology.

Cognitive scientists and linguists have long argued that by using metaphors, we can see the world in new ways. Since we have a hard time visualizing something unfamiliar, we instead take a word or concept we are familiar with and recast it into an unknown or abstract concept. We understand new things by comparing them to things we already know. This is why a control unit for a computer is called a computer mouse, a tall building is called a skyscraper, and a new pair of lightweight running shoes is called Air. Metaphors can open a new world for us by explaining how we will experience this world—or the aspects of its particular phenomena.

We all have an idea what humanities and liberal arts stand for and what computer technology stands for. But when you put the two concepts together, they shape an entirely new set of ideas: computers should be tools for creative work; computers should be beautiful; technology should be humane and joyful; user experiences matter; computing should be personal; and computers are made for normal people and not just technology nerds.

Steve Jobs used the metaphor of liberal arts and humanities to help realize his vision for Apple, opening a new world for Apple's staff, customers, and users. By calling upon this metaphor frequently, he gave the company a long-term direction for its product development, design, technology, retail outlets, business model, and brand. This direction enabled each part of the company to add to the same picture every time it created something new. He achieved the outcome that Genevieve Bell hoped (and still hopes) to realize at Intel when she began helping the company's executives narrate the story of Intel differently, namely, in terms of human experience.

Interestingly, Jobs's perspective on technology wasn't something he jammed up in a brainstorming session; neither was it a calculated business plan he deducted from analyzing the market. Being at the intersection of humanities and technology was a perspective he had thought about for a long time, something that he could sense was missing and something he wanted to see happen. So in addition to functioning as a powerful tool for narrating his company's mission, the intersection perspective also informed the company's activities and decisions. To use a term from the previous chapter, he mastered perspective-driven innovation.

You can find businesses with a strong perspective everywhere and in all shapes and sizes. General Electric, for example, has a strong perspective on using the company's creative resources to solve the world's environmental problems, a point of view it calls "ecomagination." The pharmaceutical company Novo Nordisk has a perspective on diabetes: "Changing Diabetes" aims to break the curve of the diabetes pandemic. Novo Nordisk uses this challenge to guide its investment in R&D and to develop better diabetes support, education, and self-management. It also uses its perspective to engage policy makers, patient organizations, and experts to drive diabetes awareness and prevention. Starbucks has fueled its global expansion with a strong perspective on coffee culture and the coffee shop as a "third place"—your home is the first place, your work is the second place, and Starbucks is the third place. A local soccer club in Copenhagen tells every visitor about its perspective on the game. A sign in the entrance of the club states MAKES BOYS INTO MEN AND MEN INTO BOYS. As you might guess, this club does not offer training for females. The Canadian prison system changed the very idea of what a prison is when the management developed its perspective on prison: "The prisoner shall not return." The perspective shifted the implicit metaphor from prison as a place for retention to prison as an educational institute.

Businesses that have a perspective are much better at innovating their products and services than business without. One of the reasons is that the employees across the organization share a similar mind-set about the newness the company is looking for—think of LEGO's going "back to the brick." This shared mind-set dramatically lowers the risk of failing and empowers staff on all levels to contribute with improvements that fit the overall direction.

Another reason that businesses with a strong perspective are better innovators is that they prioritize development resources for the things that matter most. Companies that lack a perspective often have very large lists of development projects in their pipeline and tend to spread their resources too thin—Coloplast's problem. This lack of focus actually increases the risk of failure because the company cannot support *any* project properly and it grows impatient with new launches. In this type of company, it is common to find hundreds of stranded projects in what is sometimes called "the graveyard of innovation."

A third reason that a strong perspective leads to more and better innovation is that different departments in the company now innovate for the same cause—as made evident by the Adidas journey. The ambition and end state make sense to people across the organization in the same way. Thus, the company can launch many types of innovation that all go in the same direction: product innovation, business model innovation, sales channel innovation, and brand innovation.

A perspective is a strong view of what you would like the future to be, or how you want your company to shape the future. Normally there are four horizons in front of you. A perspective enables you to lift your head as a leader and look out onto the furthest of the following four horizons:

1. **Yourself and your career:** This horizon is the one closest to you. At this horizon, you focus on what the company does for you, how much you earn, what career jump you can take, and what legacy you will leave. This is a very shortsighted horizon with very limited perspective.

2. **The company:** At this horizon, you ask questions focused on your company. How can the company improve its performance? How can we motivate and attract the best people? How do we organize ourselves better? This horizon has more perspective but is still limited by focusing on what goes on inside the company.

3. **Industry:** Here you worry about how the market will grow, shrink, or otherwise change. Who are the consumers, and how can we satisfy their needs? What are the growth drivers in the industry?

4. **Society:** This horizon is the furthest away from the everyday operations of the business. This horizon looks at society and the social phenomena that your company is part of. Your perspective stretches beyond the current industry boundaries and forces you to think about the very meaning of your offerings. What is our role in people's life? How can

we help make societies better? What societal shifts should we be paying attention to?

The first step to leading with perspective is to decide to have one. A surprising number of companies lack perspective. In these firms, the senior executives are mostly focused on the first or second horizon—their own career or the performance of the company. This might be fine when the business is doing well, but such a narrow perspective is insufficient to take a business out of a fog. We have never heard of a company that transformed itself or solved a very complex, uncertain situation without having a perspective that reached at least to the third horizon—the market—or even better, the fourth: the society at large. All of our examples of companies that are innovation leaders in their industry have a strong perspective on the fourth horizon.

So how do you build a perspective? Your own interpretation of the sensemaking method described in this book is a good place to start. Studying the phenomena that your business is part of will go a long way toward building a perspective. To build a perspective, however, you need to do more than just understand the current context and your customers and users. You also need to understand where the industry might be changing or should change in the future.

You cannot, of course, predict the future with 100 percent accuracy. But you can make reasonable projections by paying attention to the practices at the edge of your industry. You can observe people experimenting with new ways or extreme ways of using products. You can watch entrepreneurs who are trying to launch things that do not make sense, or you can follow ideas that are spreading in expert communities. Even the entrance of a new type of customer that usually does not belong in the normal understanding of your industry can offer insight into the future. Some of these marginal practices might become mainstream one day or might inspire your perspective on how you want the business to change.

Here are a couple of ideas of how you, as a leader, can start building a perspective on your business:

- Collect all the data and research you have on customers, markets, and the industry, and have a team synthesize the insights with the following question in mind: What do we know about why we are here? Use the synthesis to agree on what you don't know.

- Take a hard look at yourself. Look at the last five to ten product launches, and ask yourself and your team the following question: What is our point of view? Ask yourself and your team if that point of view can inspire the next five to ten product launches. If not, use the occasion to agree on the need to build a stronger perspective.

- Consider conducting a deep-dive study of behaviors, needs, and marginal practices that can give your company a new perspective. Engage people across function to participate actively in such a study.

- Use all the inspiration you can get to think about what you want to stand for as a company. Ask yourself and your team, What is our role in the world? How can we make life better for people? Write your point of view down in a short document, and use it to discuss with your team.

- Look for the right metaphor to describe the perspective, and write it down in a short statement. Look for a metaphor that is intuitively easy to understand and at the same time somehow surprising and stretches people's thinking.

Connecting Different Worlds

In his memoir, the French author Antoine de Saint-Exupéry wisely writes, "Love does not consist in gazing at each other but in looking together in the same direction."

The same idea can be applied to the task of taking a business out of a fog. *Gazing at each other,* in this context, would mean focusing on the internal aspects of the organization—the vision, core values, goals, and capabilities. *Looking in the same direction* would mean having a shared perspective and sense of discovery across the company.

Getting people across the organization to look in the same direction is easier said than done. We sometimes talk about companies as though they were a person with one common mind. But in reality, companies often consist of many different worlds and subcultures with different agendas, different cultural codes, and different metrics of success involving different career paths, different power structures, and different languages. A major challenge for the sensemaker is how to get these worlds to look in the same direction.

A good example is the world of marketing and the world of R&D. Marketing people are often generalists who tend to see the big picture—they're rewarded on short-term goals, they need to act now, and they're motivated by insights that can give them answers. R&D people, on the other hand, are very often functional specialists— they're rewarded for long-term progress, they're very focused on details and often on what new technologies can *do* rather than what is needed, and they're motivated by insights that can give them questions and puzzles to solve. Not surprisingly, these two worlds often collide. In a global consumer-goods company we recently visited, the marketing team had deliberately chosen to hold back ideas on workshops with the R&D team and expressed that "the people

from R&D don't understand the business fundamentals anyway."
Interestingly, the R&D team had come to a similar conclusion about
the marketing team: "They are so short-term focused and have no
respect for how to develop technology."

For these very reasons, most companies' R&D and marketing groups
usually follow very different agendas and directions. This becomes a
problem when you want to create a new direction for where and how
the company competes. The two worlds will probably have different
interpretations of what the future direction means for them, and you
will most likely end up with more confusion than clarity.

As a sensemaker, you need to connect worlds: to draw the eye of
the entire organization toward the same star in the sky. That means
getting divergent groups on the same page on why, how, and where
the company needs to innovate and doing so in a way that moti-
vates people, energizes the teams, and leaves lots of initiative to the
organization.

This is not just a matter of getting the message across through
a new series of commands from on high. Rather, successful sensemakers look at leadership as a conversation where people are
encouraged to participate in the interpretation of what it all means
and how anyone can put it into action. Sometimes it can even be a
good idea to ask different parts of the organization to participate
together in the discovery process before any conclusions are drawn.
In Coloplast, for example, the CEO, the marketing director, and the
R&D director went on field trips together to investigate how other
companies handled leadership and innovation. This shared sense
of discovery removed a lot of disagreements and made it easier to
implement large changes in how the company organized its innovation. At Intel, company leaders have divided their strategy process into three distinct parts: sensing, interpretation, and action.
To make the organization look in the same direction, teams of key

people from marketing, R&D, and operations work to create a shared understanding of each of these three parts:

- **Sensing:** Do we share the same insights?

- **Interpretation:** Are we making the same interpretation of what it means?

- **Action:** Do we agree on what actions we will take?

Treating a method like sensemaking as an organizational conversation as opposed to a command from on high has a number of advantages: it creates a high level of trust, it builds ownership in the organization, and it speeds up the time from insight to action. The conversation does not necessarily have to be tightly structured like a change management project. In fact, in many of the most successful companies we know, the conversation is often more loosely organized and takes place in many forums over a set period. Think of the way you marinate meat over several hours to make it tender and full of flavor: the conversation needs to simmer.

Of course, the conversation can't go on forever. Once the direction is set and everybody is on board, the sensemaker needs to shift focus from talking to acting. Now the job of leadership is to keep everyone on track and to avoid the distractions of mythical silver bullet solutions.

Building a Brain Trust

The whole point of designing the sensemaking method as an organizational conversation is to ensure that there is room for critique and critical thinking. As a leader, you cannot be sure that you are always making the right interpretations or know the right path. Therefore it is important that you build an advisory team around you to challenge your own thinking. Three roles are important in a leader's brain trust.

The *reconfigurators* are great at spotting new opportunities and inspiring the company with fresh ideas. They are excellent at conceptual thinking and at sensing new marginal practices that might change the industry. Often regarded as creative leaders, they have the rare talent of capturing and revealing new trends and opportunities. Their real skill, however, is rarely the ability to come up with new ideas themselves, but rather the ability to sense ideas, insights, and practices that are not on the company's radar and to redefine them as business opportunities. The reconfigurators ensure that the leadership team has its antennae out and is at the cutting edge of development. However, they tend to be a bit unsystematic: they can lack logic and rigor and quickly lose interest when things become too repetitive.

The *articulators* are excellent in translating new thinking into the practical, everyday activities of the company. Articulators are often quite process-oriented and will take a critical look at the feasibility of new ideas. Their role is to make sure that the organization can understand the new direction and knows how to act on it. Without the articulators in a leadership group, a new direction will easily end up as all talk and no action. Articulators tend to be very systematic and good at connecting dreamers with doers.

The *conservators* are focused on maintaining the operation of the company. Skeptical of too much change, they prioritize interventions that can bring stability to the organization. They look to reform, to get back on track, to conserve the core pillars of the company, and to make sure that new ideas can be repeated and scaled. They are fast at understanding when change is inevitable and will help diffuse the fresh ideas of the reconfigurators to the mainstream of the organization. Without conservators in a leadership team, new thinking will be hard to inject into the core of the company.

Having a balance of reconfigurators, articulators, and conservators within a leader's advisory board helps the sensemaker to avoid one-dimensional thinking. This makes it far less risky to engage in a companywide effort of navigating out of a fog. At the same time, by including these three mind-sets at a high level of conversation, the leadership increases the chances of connecting the different worlds inside the company. The resulting environment encourages the whole company to look in the same direction instead of gazing at each other.

Making Different Worlds Work for Your Company

So what can you do to connect the different worlds across your company? Here are some suggestions:

- Get a good sense of what defines the most important worlds inside the company. Be curious, for example, about how the worlds of marketing, design, sales, and R&D work and what constitutes the different ideas of success for each of them. Focus on the worlds that often are in opposition, and try to understand what is causing the discord.

- Invite executives from different worlds to be part of the discovery process, and ask them to identify their shared insights.

- Look at the sensemaking method as a corporate conversation that occurs within a set time frame. Encourage people across the organization to contribute. Be open for suggestions and ideas while the process is going on, but be clear that the conversation has a window that closes at a certain point.

- Consider if you have the right balance of roles in your advisory group. Do you have people focused on bringing fresh thinking, people who can translate ideas into action, and people who can stabilize the business?

Getting People Right

I F YOU HAVE JUST ONE single takeaway from our book, we hope it is this: getting people right is the key to taking your business out of a fog.

If it were that easy, however, this book would only be one page long! By default, most of us get people wrong quite often—especially when we are trying to make sharp shifts in strategy. As has been argued throughout the book, most of us take for granted various assumptions about customers and users when we create business strategy or solve problems around marketing, product innovation, and sales. These assumptions are generalizations about human behavior and have very little to do with how people really experience the world.

These potentially unhelpful assumptions include the following:

- Human beings, first and foremost, are individual, thinking beings.

- We are fully aware of our intentions.

- Our choices are informed by weighing different options against each other.

- We know what we want and need.

- We are the same, regardless of the social context or mood we are in.

When the business environment is relatively stable, these assumptions help us to create economies of scale and to run an efficient and smooth business. We don't have to think about what really guides our customers' behavior every time we make a business decision. But when we are confronted with a sudden shift in the business environment, it's time to dismantle these habits of mind. The human sciences provide the theoretical scaffolding that helps us get people right:

- Human beings are, first and foremost, social creatures.

- We make most of our decisions according to our familiarity with the world.

- We change our preferences according to the mood and social setting we are in.

- Our choices are often made spontaneously.

- We are at our best when we are fully engaged in the world.

If you tacitly assume that your customers make decisions by weighing options, you will end up adding features to your products that nobody understands or needs. If you assume that humans are, primarily, optimizing individuals, not bound by social code and structure, you will not understand how new categories are created and diffused into the mass market. If you assume that your customers are fully aware of their needs and intentions, you will continue launching products that lack interest or excitement.

Where Do I Start?

The big question, of course, is where and how you start if you want to get people right in your own organization. To begin with, it's important that you see a method like sensemaking as a journey rather than another research technique in your marketing research toolbox. Lots of companies have already embraced the research techniques that we have introduced in this book—ethnographic fieldwork, for example. These can be great if you want to create better designs and user interfaces or if you want to understand how your customers interact with products. But the research technique doesn't bring any significant value in and of itself, and it certainly doesn't bring you out of a fog unless you know how to apply it into a larger strategic vision. Ethnographic research should be viewed as one of many small wheels in a bigger machine that is designed to set your direction and future.

The value of mastering sensemaking exists in what you make of your insights, how you translate these insights into new ideas and opportunities, how you create a shared perspective on your business, how you use the insights to prioritize initiatives, and how you execute on the direction you find. All these elements must constitute the main narrative of your business agenda; they can't be relegated to a subplot.

We believe that the best first step is to create a crisp and clear problem frame that precisely targets the issues you are dealing with and, at the same time, encourages curiosity and discovery: *reframe the problem as a phenomenon.* If your team can create a shared understanding of the problem and agree on what you and the rest of the team don't know, it is much easier to accept *new* ways of solving the problem. A good way to do this is to involve your colleagues in spotting signs that your company might be in a fog. Use the following questions to guide the conversation:

- What is our long-term perspective on our business? Is it clear and inspiring?

- Do we know where future growth will come from?

- Are we creating excitement in the market?

- Do we understand the changes that are going on in the periphery of our industry?

- Are we good at spotting and acting on changes in the market?

- Are we creating demand, or are we following needs?

Another good way of communicating the need for getting people right is to work with your team on illuminating the assumptions you are making about your customers. A useful starting point is to collect all the research that your company has done on customers over the last five years and map what you know and don't know. A more sophisticated method is to audit your current proposition to your customers. Look at all the points where your customers come in touch with your products and offerings, and try to understand what you are really selling them. Use this to discuss the following questions:

- Who are our customers?

- What are we helping our customers achieve?

- How do they experience our offerings?

- Do we know the logic of how customers adapt to new products?

- What will inspire and excite customers?

- What don't we know about our customers?

None of this will be easy. Changing our minds and our habits never is. Open-ended theories and tools from the human sciences, a rejection of long-held beliefs about the way people think and behave, an embrace of a method like sensemaking—all these steps will be counterintuitive to people in an organization steeped in the culture of business school training. Be prepared: this won't be an easy sell in your team or with your upper management. We can't promise you three easy steps to success or a magic algorithm for the solution to your business challenges, but we can promise you a journey toward an understanding of how your customers actually experience life. This is the only journey that can deliver the moments that change everything: moments of clarity.

GLOSSARY

abductive reasoning, p. 102

A method of reasoning based on the formation and evaluation of hypotheses using the best available information and nonlinear problem solving. A practical, problem-solving application of abductive reasoning is **sensemaking**.

attunement, definition p. 99

A key social skill that enables us to get in sync with a particular **world** and learn its rules—that is, its customs and practices—in order to switch fluidly between worlds.

behavioral economics, p. 3

A field within economics that includes social and psychological factors in models of economic decision making, with a particular focus on the difference between rational and irrational decisions.

care (*sorge*), p. 166

Martin Heidegger (1889–1976), a German philosopher known for his existential and phenomenological explorations, used the word "care" (from the German, *sorge*), not in the sense of an explicit emotional connection with things or people, but in the sense that something matters or is deeply meaningful to an individual. It is this "care" that enables individuals to see new and complex ways of interacting with the world.

confirmation bias, p. 40

A tendency for people to listen to, accept, or believe information that supports their existing beliefs. Confirmation bias can lead people to selectively interpret data or ignore counterexamples. When it works to change how people remember facts or events, it is called confirmatory memory, p. XX

deductive logic, p. 13

See entry for **deductive reasoning**.

deductive reasoning, p. 102

The deriving of a conclusion by reasoning; specifically, reasoning in which the conclusion about particulars follows necessarily from general or universal premises. See entry for **hypothesis-driven problem solving**.

default thinking, p. 12

> Based on deductive reasoning, default thinking is an approach that addresses
> a problem using linear and rational problem solving. Typically it involves
> the quantitative analysis of large sets of data. Its strength lies in its ability to
> address business challenges that demand an increase in the productivity of
> a system, but it is less successful at addressing challenges involving human
> behavior.

design thinking, p. 57

> Applying useful ways of thinking about the design process—specifically,
> a mixture of empathy, creativity, and rationality—to larger creative and
> analytical projects.

ethnography, p. 88; definition, p. 90

> An in-depth approach to researching cultures that involves immersing oneself in
> a particular society rather than focusing on proving or disproving a hypothesis.
> As a research method, ethnography involves the process of observing,
> documenting, and then analyzing human behavior within a specific cultural
> context. It is one of the main data collection techniques for the **human sciences**.

existential psychology, p. 14

> A branch of psychology that incorporates existentialist philosophy into the
> study of human psychology. It sees motivation as more than simply mechanisms
> and drives and includes the individual's will and desire in its lexicon.

habitus, p. 39

> An all-encompassing mind-set, influenced by an individual's background (e.g.,
> family, class position, educational and occupational status), activities, and
> experiences of everyday life, that unconsciously determines that individual's
> tastes, preferences, and habits.

hermeneutics

> A set of methods and principles for interpreting verbal and nonverbal
> communication.

human sciences, definition, p. 4

> A group of scientific disciplines that focus on understanding how humans
> experience the world. By looking at **aspects** of the world that are subject to
> human experience, the human sciences stand apart from the physical sciences
> (such as chemistry and physics), which focus on **properties**. The human
> sciences include disciplines such as anthropology, sociology, and psychology, as
> well as art, philosophy, and literature. See entry for **properties and aspects**.

hypothesis-driven problem solving, p. 127

> The primary method used for **deductive reasoning**. Hypotheses are tested
> with the data at hand, and conclusions are drawn from the validation of the
> hypotheses. The goal is to find the "right" solution, which means that the
> question of whether this is the "right" problem to solve is overlooked.

inductive reasoning, p. 102

> A method of reasoning based on generalizations derived from a set of specific
> observations. However, since inductive reasoning is limited by an individual's own
> belief system it is not useful for problems involving human behavior and culture.

instrumental rationalism, p. 26

A paradigm that assumes that business problems can be solved through objective and scientific analysis and that evidence and facts should prevail over opinions and preferences. Instrumental rationalism gives rise to the type of default problem-solving model (or **default thinking**) that dominates the business world.

logical positivism, p. 29

A more extreme version of **positivism**, logical positivism claims that the physical world and human society can be explained in terms of general laws of logic and linguistics.

marginal practices, p. 76

Ways in which people interact with each other, or with technology, that aren't accounted for in mainstream culture or in a business's current strategy. Looking at marginal practices can identify people's unmet needs—both from other people and from technology—and point to areas for future innovation.

meaningful distinctions, p. 154

See entry for **perspective-driven innovation**.

nonlinear problem solving, p. 105

The antithesis of linear problem solving, nonlinear problem solving involves a higher level of intentionality and objective analysis and defeats the bias innate in linear problem solving. The term is also used synonymously with **abductive reasoning**.

panopticon, p. 120

A type of institutional building that became popular in the late eighteenth century. The concept of the design is to allow a watchman to constantly observe inmates of an institution without their knowledge. The panopticon has been invoked as a metaphor for modern "disciplinary" societies that use surveillance as a method of control.

paradigm shift, p. 77

A shift in the basic assumptions that make up a philosophical or theoretical framework governing a branch of science, technology, or business. The development of plate tectonics is an example from geology; the move to microelectronics is an example from technology.

perspective-driven innovation, p. 134

Innovation based on making **meaningful distinctions** between what matters and has meaning to a company and what does not. Meaningful distinctions considered together produce a perspective. This perspective drives the process of developing ideas, strategies, and products for the company, in addition to defining the company's mission.

phenomenology, definition p. 78

The "science of phenomena" or the study of how people experience life. Whereas the hard sciences analyze the "property" data points of a given phenomenon, phenomenology focuses on its experiential "aspects." Phenomenology focuses in particular on the relationships between people and objects, rather than on the essence of the object itself. It is a core approach in the **human sciences**. See entry for **properties and aspects**.

phenomenon, p. 79
> A fact or event that is observed to exist or happen, especially one whose cause is in question. Any phenomenon can be analyzed using "property" data points from the hard sciences or experiential "aspects" from **phenomenology**.

positivism, p. 28
> The belief that scientific knowledge—and only scientific knowledge—can explain human society, just as it explains the physical world. Positivism rejects intuitive knowledge and claims that, just as gravity governs the physical world, general and measurable laws govern society.

practice, p. 77
> An activity that requires learning and rehearsal. The key practice in this book is **sensemaking**.

problem scale, p. 23
> Used by anthropologists, this term refers to the levels of complexity of a given problem, ranging from simple problems with known solutions to those that become increasingly complex and confounding.

properties and aspects, p. 79
> An object has properties that are the same regardless of how humans experience them. For example, a property of a hammerhead is that it is made up of iron molecules. An object also has aspects, which are subject to human experience. For example, an aspect of a hammerhead is that it is hard to the touch. To use another example, if biological gender—male or female—is a property, then cultural gender—masculine or feminine—is an aspect.

qualitative analysis, p. 44
> An approach to understanding human behavior that is interpretative rather than objective, qualitative analysis uses ethnographic techniques, usually involving interviews and participation in a phenomenon, to look for drivers of a behavior that cannot be quantified. Qualitative analysis seeks to understand the underlying meanings and motivations of human behavior. It is very powerful at identifying and understanding new and unexplained behaviors.

quantitative analysis, p. 41
> An approach to understanding human behavior that seeks to achieve the objectivity of the natural sciences by breaking down a phenomenon into discrete and measurable variables. Quantitative analysis uses surveys and other techniques to quantify people's behavior based on numbers and percentages, which can then be analyzed using statistics. Sample size is very important. If the sample is sufficiently large, quantitative analysis can be a powerful tool in providing an understanding of the size and extent of a phenomenon that has already been identified.

rational actor, p. 140
> Within an economic system, an individual who pursues goals that reflect his or her own perceived self-interest, and these preferences are consistent and

stable. If given options, a rational actor will choose the option with the highest expected utility.

scenario planning, p. 25

The use of hypothetical scenarios to "rehearse the future" and guide planning for expansion strategies or business continuity models.

sensemaking, p. 14

A nonlinear process for solving complex problems that are hard to conceptualize and articulate. Based in the **human sciences**, sensemaking is exploratory rather than confirmatory. It seeks to address why-based rather than hypothesis-based questions in contexts of high uncertainty using qualitative data. It is a five-step process:

1. Frame the problem as a **phenomenon**.
2. Collect the data.
3. Look for patterns.
4. Create the key insights.
5. Build the business impact.

Taylorism, p. 29

An early form of management science that defined a company as a system made up of workflows to be improved. Under this theory, efficiency, standardization, and measurement are the key tools for improving the management of a company.

thick description, definition p. 95

Coined by the anthropologist Clifford Geertz, a thick description of a particular human behavior not only describes the behavior but seeks to make sense of it by studying it within its own cultural context. By doing this, the behavior becomes meaningful to an outsider. Thick description is an important ethnographic technique.

thinking outside the box, p. 57

The practice of looking at problems in unconventional ways and coming up with ideas that are new, fresh, and unexpected. The "box" in business discourse refers to the conventional frame—the normal way of thinking—including a firm's organizational routines, processes, practices, and existing ideas. Thinking outside the box, then, entails deviating from this normal way of thinking. It is the antithesis of **default thinking**.

trend spotting, p. 25

The identification of broad trends in consumer behavior or technological adoption that point to needs that are going unmet by the current market. See entry for **marginal practices**.

world, definition p. 98

An all-encompassing system created by the people within it and connected by its own unique set of equipment, rules, practices, social norms, and terminology; for example, "the business world," "the theatre world," or "the world of high finance."

NOTES

INTRODUCTION

p. 3:   **fueled by the myth:** This myth is routed in Western metaphysics, especially René Descartes's grounding of us as being thinking things: René Descartes, *Meditations on First Philosophy,* 3rd ed. (Indianapolis: Hackett, 1993).

CHAPTER ONE: NAVIGATING IN A FOG

p. 9:   **quadrupled their size since the 1980s:** Kevin Spence, "Nike by the Numbers," *Gatton Student Research Publication* 1, no. 1 (2009) (Gatton College of Business and Economics, University of Kentucky); see also www.fundinguniverse.com., including "Puma AG Rudolf Dassler Sports History," Funding Universe webpage, accessed July 15, 2013, www .fundinguniverse.com/company-histories/puma-ag-rudolf-dassler-sport-history; and "New Balance Athletic Shoe Inc., History," Funding Universe Web page, accessed July 15, 2013, www.fundinguniverse.com/company-histories/new-balance-athletic-shoe-inc-history.

p. 10:   **more than half of the entire sporting goods market:** National Sporting Goods Association, *Sports Participation in the United States 2012* and *Sports Participation Single Sport 2012,* research reports, accessed July 15, 2012, www.nsga.org/i4a/pages/index.cfm?pageid=4653.See also M. Kilpatrick, E. Hebert, and J. Bartholomew, "College Students' Motivation for Physical Activity: Differentiating Men's and Women's Motives for Sport Participation and Exercise," *Journal of American College Health* 54, no. 2 (September–October 2005): 87–94.

p. 10:   **baseball shoes was decreasing:** Ibid.

p. 10:   **50 percent of demand for sports products:** Ibid.

p. 10:   **According to a recent study:** Ibid.

CHAPTER TWO: BUSINESS ANALYSIS, DATA, AND LOGIC

p. 22:   **approaching a new "age of discontinuity":** Peter Drucker, *The Age of Discontinuity: Guidelines to Our Changing Society* (New York: Harper & Row, 1969), ii.

p. 22:   **his best-selling book *Future Shock*:** Alvin Toffler, *Future Shock* (New York: Bantam Books, 1990), 2.

p. 22:   **1973 book *Beyond the Stable State*:** Donald Schon, *Beyond the Stable State* (New York: Norton, 1973).

p. 23:   **a late stage of "modernity":** Anthony Giddens, *The Consequences of Modernity* (Palo Alto: Stanford University Press, 1990); Ulrich Beck, *Risk Society: Towards a New Modernity* (Thousand Oaks, CA: Sage Publications, 1992).

p. 23:   **change management:** Tom Peters, *Liberation Management: Necessary Disorganization for the Nanosecond Nineties* (New York: A. A. Knopf, 1992); Gary Hamel, *Leading the Revolution: How to Thrive in Turbulent Times by Making Innovation a Way of Life,* rev. ed. (Boston: Harvard Business Review Press, 2002).

p. 28:   **The founding father of management science:** Matthew Stewart, *The Management Myth: Debunking Modern Business Philosophy* (New York: W. W. Norton & Company, 2010), offers an entertaining description of Taylor's original experiments.

p. 29:   **Taylorism:** Frederick Winslow Taylor, *The Principles of Scientific Management* (New York and London: Norton, 1911), 26.

p. 30:   **A famous study by the Swedish psychologist:** Ola Svenson, "Are We Less Risky and More Skillful Than Our Fellow Drivers?" *Acta Psychologic,* February 1981, 47(2): 143–148.

p. 30:   **A similar study some years later:** Ulrike Malmendier and Geoffrey Tate, "Does Overconfidence Affect Corporate Investment? CEO Overconfidence Measures Revisited," *European Financial Management* 11, no. 5 (2005): 649–659.

p. 31:   **more than $18 billion was spent:** Jo Bowman, "A World of Difference: ESOMAR Global Market Research 2012," September 13, 2012, http://rwconnect.esomar.org/2012/09/13/a-world-of-difference-esomar-global-market-research-2012/.

p. 31:   **We did an interesting experiment:** ReD Associates, unpublished research.

p. 32:   **Even studies of people with written shopping:** Robert S. Wieder, "Impulse Marketing: How Supermarkets Help Make Us Fat," CalorieLab, November 2012, http://calorielab.com/news/2012/11/08/impulse-marketing-how-supermarkets-help-make-us-fat/.

p. 34:   **a 2006 article in the McKinsey Quarterly:** Ian Davis and Elizabeth Stephenson, "Ten Investment Trends for the Future," *McKinsey Quarterly,* Q1, January 2006.

p. 35:   book *How Brands Grow*: Byron Sharp, *How Brands Grow: What Marketers Don't Know* (New York: Oxford University Press, 2010).

p. 35:   **psychologist Paco Underhill uncovers**: Paco Underhill, *Why We Buy: The Science of Shopping* (New York: Simon and Schuster: 2007).

p. 35:   **writer Kevin Hogan tells us**: Kevin Hogan, *The Science of Influence* (New York: Wiley, 2010).

p. 35:   **the authors of the article "Better Branding"**: Nora A. Aufreiter, David Elzinga, and Jonathan W. Gordon, "Better Branding," *McKinsey Quarterly,* November 2003, www.mckinsey.com/insights/marketing_sales/better_branding.

p. 36:   **According to an article in the *Washington Post***: Margaret Webb Pressler, "Low-Carb Fad Fades, and Atkins Is Big Loser," *Washington Post,* August 2, 2005, www.washingtonpost.com/wp-dyn/content/article/2005/08/02/AR2005080200276.html.

p. 37:   **By 2004, the market for low-carb diet food**: Melanie Warner, "Is the Low-Carb Boom Over?" *New York Times,* December 5, 2004, www.nytimes.com/2004/12/05/business/yourmoney/05atki.html?pagewanted=all&position=.

p. 39:   **coined the term *habitus***: Pierre Bourdieu, *Distinction: A Social Critique of the Judgement of Taste* (Cambridge, MA: Harvard University Press, 1984), 170.

p. 40:   **Cognitive psychologists call this *confirmation bias***: Charles G. Lord, Lee Ross, and Mark R. Lepper, "Biased Assimilation and Attitude Polarization: The Effects of Prior Theories on Subsequently Considered Evidence," *Journal of Personality and Social Psychology* 37, no. 11 (1979): 2,098–2,109.

p. 40:   **psychologists refer to as *confirmatory memory***: Reid Hastie and Bernadette Park, "The Relationship Between Memory and Judgment Depends on Whether the Judgment Task Is Memory-Based or On-Line," in *Social Cognition: Key Readings,* ed. David L. Hamilton (New York: Psychology Press, 2005), 394.

p. 41:   **Leo Tolstoy's nonfiction magnum opus**: Leo Tolstoy, *The Kingdom of God Is Within You,* trans. Constance Garnett (New York, 1894). Project Gutenberg edition released November 2002, www.gutenberg.org/cache/epub/4602/pg4602.html.

p. 42:   **Roger Martin**: Roger Martin, "Beyond the Numbers: Building Your Qualitative Intelligence," *Harvard Business Review,* May 1, 2010.

p. 45:   **Jürgen Habermas**: Jürgen Habermas, *The Theory of Communicative Action,* vol. 2, *Lifeworld and Systems: A Critique of Functionalist Reason* (Cambridge & Oxford: Polity Press, 1991).

p. 46:   **This complex and esoteric terminology**: Allen C. Smith III and Sherryl Kleinman, "Managing Emotions in Medical School: Students' Contacts with the Living and the Dead," *Social Psychology Quarterly,* 52, no. 1 (1989): 56–69.

CHAPTER THREE: GETTING CREATIVE!

p. 59: **Alex F. Osborn:** Alex Faickney Osborn, *Your Creative Power: How to Use Imagination* (Myers Press, 2007).

p. 59: **"Each of us does have an Aladdin's lamp":** Ibid., 8.

p. 59: **"Brainstorming means":** Ibid., 265.

p. 60: **You can't solve two problems in one session:** Ibid., 265.

p. 61: **the author of *Weird Ideas That Work*:** Robert Sutton, *Weird Ideas That Work* (New York: Free Press, 2007), 147.

p. 61: **writes Michael Michalko:** Michael Michalko, "Thinking Like a Genius," *The Futurist,* May 1998.

p. 63: **writes in his best-seller *Leading the Revolution*:** Gary Hamel, *Leading the Revolution: How to Thrive in Turbulent Times by Making Innovation a Way of Life* (Boston: Harvard Business Review Press, 2002), 23.

p. 63: **"you are already irrelevant":** Ibid., 72.

p. 63: **asks his readers to give an oath:** Ibid., 23.

p. 64: **author of *How to Have Kick-Ass Ideas*:** Chris Baréz-Brown, *How to Have Kick-Ass Ideas: Shake Up Your Business, Shake Up Your Life* (New York: Skyhorse, 2008), 17.

p. 64: **"say '*Na na na-na na*' and laugh at the world":** Ibid., 86.

p. 65: **"clever clever thinky thinky" people:** Ibid., 55.

p. 66: **a series of mind riddles:** M. C. Orman, "How Einstein Arrived at E = MC Squared," the Health Resource Network, http://www.stresscure.com/hrn/einstein.html.

p. 67: **Mihaly Csikszentmihalyi's famous studies:** Mihaly Csikszentmihalyi, *Creativity: Flow and the Psychology of Discovery and Invention* (New York: Harper Perennial, 1997).

p. 67: **"Cognitive accounts of what happens during":** Ibid., 101.

CHAPTER FOUR: THE HUMAN SCIENCES

p. 78: **Phenomenology is the study of how people:** Martin Heidegger, *Being and Time* (New York: Harper Perennial Modern Classics, 2008), 50.

p. 79: **rather will show the essence of our *relationship* to that thing:** Ibid., 53.

p. 79: **through the use of *correctness*:** Martin Heidegger, *The Question Concerning Technology and Other Essays* (New York and London: Garland Publishing, 1977), 42.

p. 80: **our familiarity—our act of *being*—in the world:** Heidegger, *Being and Time,* 78.

p. 80: **We are not conscious of:** Ibid., 91–122.

p. 81: **The slogan of phenomenology is "to the things themselves":** Edmund Husserl, *Logical Investigations* (New York: Springer, 2003), 168.

p. 83: **After the publication of her first books, Alice Munro:** She describes this experience in the introduction to her collection: Alice Munro, *Selected Stories* (New York: Vintage Contemporaries, 1996), xiii–xv.

p. 83:   "brass tacks" information about the writing life: Ibid., xiii.

p. 83:   It assumes that I am a person of brisk intelligence: Ibid.

p. 84:   "I would try to make lists": Alice Munro, *The Lives of Girls and Women* (New York: Vintage, 2001), 276.

p. 84:   Twyla Tharp described: Twyla Tharp with Mark Reiter, *Twyla Tharp: The Creative Habit* (New York: Simon and Schuster, 2003), 65.

p. 85:   Toshio Odate: Bill Wellman, "The Feel, the Smell, the Art of Working with Wood," *New York Times,* September 26, 1999, www.nytimes.com/1999/09/26/nyregion/the-feel-the-smell-the-art-of-working-with-wood.html.

p. 85:   Terence Blanchard: Jeffrey Hyatt, "Talkin' Miles: Photos, Documentaries and Quotes," Miles Davis Online, July 9, 2009, http://milesdavis.wordpress.com/2009/07/09/talkin-miles-photos-documentaries-quotes/.

p. 85:   Davis himself put it simply: Ibid.

p. 86:   all the way back to Plato: Plato, *The Republic, Book VII,* The Internet Classics Archive, accessed July 15, 2013, http://classics.mit.edu/Plato/republic.9.viii.html.

p. 86:   Descartes was the philosopher: René Descartes, *Meditations on First Philosophy* (Indianapolis: Hackett, 1993).

p. 87:   we are "beings in the world": Heidegger, *Being and Time,* 11.

p. 88:   Bruno Latour's ethnographic description: Bruno Latour, *Laboratory Life* (Princeton, NJ: Princeton University Press, 1986), 16.

p. 90:   "The integration of all the details observed": Bronisław Malinowski, *Argonauts of the Western Pacific* (Malinowski Press, 2007), 84.

p. 92:   Notes from the Field: Eliot Salandy Brown, "Observing China Through People: An Ethnographer's Notes from the Field," ReD Associates website, accessed July 15, 2013, http://tinyurl.com/lx7t7hv.

p. 95:   famously describes as *thick description*: Clifford Geertz, *The Interpretation of Cultures* (New York: Basic Books, 1977), 1.

p. 96:   Adele: Thick and Thin: Parts of this section appeared in Morgan Ramsey-Elliot, "The Anti-Anatomy of a Tearjerker," ReD Associates website, accessed July 15, 2013, www.redassociates.com/conversations/sense-making/adele-and-the-anti-anatomy-of-a-tearjerker/.

p. 96:   "Chill-provoking passages": Michaeleen Doucleff, "Anatomy of a Tear-Jerker," *Wall Street Journal,* February 11, 2012, http://online.wsj.com/article/SB1000:14240529702036460045772130102917901378.html.

p. 96:   recent *Saturday Night Live* skit: *Saturday Night Live,* NBC, season 37, episode 1604, November 12, 2011, www.nbc.com/saturday-night-live/recaps/#cat=37&mea=1604&ima=112393.

p. 99:   Attunement: Martin Heidegger, *Being and Time* (New York: Harper Perennial Modern Classics, 2008), 176.

p. 101:   chains of meaning: *in order to*: Ibid., 97–122.

p. 102:   Charles Sanders Peirce became famous: Charles Sanders Peirce, "Pragmatism as the Logic of Abduction," in *The Essential Peirce,* vol. 2, *Selected Philosophical Writings, 1893–1913* (Bloomington: Indiana University Press, 1998), 226–258.

p. 103:   "The abductive suggestion comes to us": Ibid., 227.

p. 103:   "Do not block the way of inquiry": Ibid., 48.

p. 104:   "Doubt is an uneasy and dissatisfied state": Charles Sanders Peirce, "The Fixation of Belief," *Popular Science Monthly* 12 (November 1877): 1–15, www.peirce.org/writings/p107.html.

CHAPTER FIVE: THE TURNAROUND

p. 108:   In the 1930s, Danish carpenter Ole Kirk Christiansen: Information on the LEGO company in this introduction was from LEGO Group, "About Us: Timeline 2000:–2010," accessed July 15, 2013, http://aboutus.lego.com/en-us/lego-group/the_lego_history/2000/.

p. 108:   the Best Toy of the Century award *twice*: LEGO Group, "Company Profile: Toy of the Century," accessed July 15, 2003, http://cache.lego .com/upload/contentTemplating/LEGOAboutUs-PressReleases/otherfiles/download177A5FCDC839AA3548FABB89C53C45AB.pdf.

p. 120:   LEGO kits from 12,900 to 7,000: "Lego's Turnaround: Picking Up the Pieces," *Economist,* October 26, 2006.

p. 120:   Executive vice president Mads Nipper described LEGO's value proposition: Diane Mehta, "Mads Nipper, Executive VP at the LEGO Group, on the Future of the Play Experience," ReD website, accessed July 17, 2013, www .redassociates.com/conversations/enabling-innovation/mads-nipper-executive-vp-at-the-lego-group-on-the-future-of-the-play-experience/.

CHAPTER SIX: PRODUCT DESIGN

p. 125:   missed its sales targets four times in *one year*: Coloplast 2009 Annual Report, accessed July 15, 2013, www.coloplast.com/Investor-Relations/Annual-reports/.

CHAPTER SEVEN: CORPORATE STRATEGY

p. 145:   The story of Adi Dassler, founder of Adidas: Adidas Group company website, accessed July 17, 2013, www.adidas-group.com/en/ourgroup/history/history.aspx.

CHAPTER EIGHT: HOW TO LEAD TO YOUR MOMENT OF CLARITY

p. 158:   in 2007, following their sensemaking process: Rob Meade, "Samsung Is Still the World's Number One TV Maker," *Techradar,* July 12, 2007, www.techradar.com/news/television/samsung-is-still-the-world-s-no-1-tv-maker-167661. See also "Samsung Hits Record High in Global TV Market Share," *What Hi-Fi?,* September 12, 2012, www.whathifi.com/news/samsung-hits-record-high-in-global-tv-market-share.

p. 163:   "perfectly ordinary, empirical, and quasi-aesthetic": Isaiah Berlin, *The Sense of Reality* (New York: Farrar, Straus and Giroux, 1999), 46.

p. 163:   "a vast amalgam of constantly changing multicolored": Ibid.

p. 163:   "direct, almost sensuous contact": Ibid.

p. 163:   "acute sense of what fits with what": Ibid.

p. 163:   "wisdom, imaginative understanding, insight or perceptiveness": Ibid.

p. 166:   or what he called *sorge*: Martin Heidegger, *Being and Time* (New York: Harper Perennial Modern Classics, 2008), 225–228.

p. 167:   his book *Testament of a Furniture Dealer*: Ingvar Kamprad, "Testament of a Furniture Dealer: A Little IKEA Dictionary," Inter IKEA Systems B.V., 2007, 15, accessed July 17, 2013, www.emu.dk/erhverv/merkantil_caseeksamen/doc/ikea/english_testament_2007.pdf.

p. 168:   interview with an epic soccer player like Lionel "Leo" Messi: "Lionel Messi Interview," *World Soccer*, January 2013, www.worldsoccer.com/features/lionel-messi-interview-part-two#UZbV7vM53JpShXaX.99.

p. 170:   "I always thought of myself as a humanities person as a kid": Walter Isaacson, *Steve Jobs* (New York: Simon & Schuster, 2011), 28.

p. 176:   the French author Antoine de Saint-Exupéry wisely writes: Antoine de Saint-Exupéry, *Wind, Sand and Stars* (New York: Harcourt Brace, 1967), 143.

INDEX

ABOUT THE AUTHORS

ReD Associates, one of the world's most progressive and forward-thinking consulting firms, is a leading force in bringing human-science-based methodologies to businesses. ReD's consultants, based primarily in New York City and Copenhagen, have worked with groups of consumers, users, and customers from all around the world, combining business analysis from traditional business practices with the tools of human-science research.

With a client list that includes the most senior management of companies like Adidas, Carlsberg, Coloplast, Intel, LEGO, Novo Nordisk, Mars, Orange, Pernod Ricard, Samsung, and Vodafone, ReD Associates has quickly garnered a reputation worldwide for helping companies solve problems in the midst of uncertainty and rapidly changing markets.

Christian Madsbjerg, one of the founding partners of ReD associates, is a key player in making the humanities and social sciences useful tools for business. Based in New York City, Madsbjerg holds a specialist role at ReD as director of client relations, where he focuses on methodologies for rigorously studying human behavior. Madsbjerg advises the executive suite of many *Fortune* 300 companies on top-level strategic issues, integrating sophisticated techniques traditionally used in academia to each company's problem-solving processes. His work has had a significant impact in the market for each of his clients.

Madsbjerg writes, teaches, and speaks all over the world. He is the author of several books on social theory, discourse analysis, and politics. He studied philosophy and political science in Copenhagen and London and has a master's degree from the University of London.

Mikkel B. Rasmussen, one of the founding partners of ReD Associates, is an expert in innovation and business creativity. As the director of ReD Associates Europe, he works closely with the top management of some of Europe's most forward-looking companies, including Adidas, LEGO, and Novo Nordisk. His work has led to several breakthrough technologies and products in the markets for toys, sporting goods, and health care. In his practice at ReD, Rasmussen has pioneered new thinking on how to make social-science methodology practical, creative, and effective in business.

Rasmussen is a well-known keynote speaker and provocateur on innovation, business creativity, and the practical use of social science. He has written numerous articles for both academic audiences and the popular press in Europe. He holds a master's degree in administration and economics from Roskilde University Denmark and a degree in the management of innovation from Maastrict University, Holland.